Unwin Education Books

DEVELOPING A CURRICULUM
A Practical Guide

Unwin Education Books

Unwin Education Books
Series Editor: Ivor Morrish

Developing a Curriculum
A Practical Guide

AUDREY NICHOLLS
Ulster Polytechnic

S. HOWARD NICHOLLS
Queen's University, Belfast

London
GEORGE ALLEN & UNWIN
Boston   Sydney

© George Allen & Unwin (Publishers) Ltd, 1972, 1978

George Allen & Unwin (Publishers) Ltd,
40 Museum Street, London WC1A 1LU, UK

George Allen & Unwin (Publishers) Ltd,
Park Lane, Hemel Hempstead, Herts HP2 4TE, UK

Allen & Unwin Inc.,
9 Winchester Terrace, Winchester, Mass 01890, USA

George Allen & Unwin Australia Pty Ltd,
8 Napier Street, North Sydney, NSW 2060, Australia

First published in 1972
Sixth impression 1976
Second edition 1978
Fourth impression 1983

British Library Cataloguing in Publication Data

Nicholls, Audrey
  Developing a curriculum. – New ed. – (Unwin
  education books; 12).
  1. Curriculum planning
  I. Title   II. Nicholls, Stanley Howard
  III. Series
  375'.001   LB1570   77–30599
  ISBN 0–04–371053–0

Printed in Great Britain by
Billing & Sons Ltd, Worcester

To Our Daughter Kay

Acknowledgements

We are very grateful to the following friends and
colleagues, all concerned with education in various
capacities, who read the manuscript and made many
helpful comments and suggestions: J. J. Campbell,
Gordon Cowan, Bill Dempsey, Frank and
Marjorie Jackson, Norman Masson, Allan Rudd and
Joan and Arnold Slaney.

In addition, one of us is particularly indebted to
Dr Allan Rudd for encouraging thinking and reading in
the field of curriculum development.

We hasten to add that the above-named do not
necessarily share the views expressed in the book.

We are also grateful to the Schools Council for
permission to reproduce an extract from their Working
Paper No. 10, *Curriculum Development: Teachers'
Groups and Centres* (H.M.S.O., 1967).

Finally, our thanks are due to Irene Barron who typed the manuscript.

Contents

Glossary of Terms Used in the Text

affective	related to feelings
aim	a statement in general terms indicating what it is hoped will be achieved
behaviour	that which pupils do, from which thinking or feelings may be inferred, or which may be an end in itself
behavioural objective	a statement indicating what pupils should be able to do as a result of learning opportunities presented
cognitive	related to knowing
course	a series of planned units related to each other
curriculum	all the opportunities planned by teachers for pupils
curriculum development	the planning of learning opportunities intended to bring about certain desired changes in pupils, and the assessment of the extent to which these changes have taken place
curriculum process	a continuous cycle of activities in which all elements of the curriculum are considered and interrelated
experience	the total mental phenomena directly received at any given time
learning opportunity	a planned and controlled relationship between pupils, teacher, materials, equipment and the environment, in which it is hoped that desired learning will take place
situation	the overall environment which includes pupils, teachers, school and locality
unit	a number of related learning opportunities

Chapter 1

The Need for
Curriculum Development

The term curriculum development is a fairly new one in the educational language of this country although it is now being used with increasing frequency. The activity implied by the term is one which a small number of thoughtful and gifted teachers have always carried out, an activity which is now slowly becoming accepted as part of the professional responsibility of all teachers.

The purpose of this book is to explain what is meant by curriculum development and what is involved in curriculum planning. It outlines the relationship among the various elements in the curriculum and explains the factors which influence it.

Its purpose is not to suggest to teachers either what or how they should be teaching their pupils. It will not discuss, for instance, the desirability of teaching a foreign language to all pupils in secondary schools or of introducing vertical grouping or the integrated day into primary schools. Decisions such as these are best made by the teachers in the schools on the basis of a complete set of evidence which only they are in a position to collect. It is hoped, however, that what this book will do is to help teachers to establish a logical process which will enable them to build a curriculum which at any given time is the best one they can provide for their pupils. It will also indicate the factors which influence the curriculum and which, therefore, need to be taken into account in curriculum planning.

WHAT IS CURRICULUM DEVELOPMENT?

Teachers need to establish very clearly what they are trying to achieve with their pupils, then to decide how they hope to do this and finally to consider to what extent they have been successful in their attempts. In other words, the planning of learning opportunities intended to bring about certain changes in pupils and the assessment of the extent to which these changes have taken place is what is meant by curriculum development. The Schools Council's Working Paper No. 10 sees this as involving four stages:

(*a*) The careful examination, drawing on all available sources of knowledge and informed judgement, of the *objectives* of teaching, whether in particular subject courses or over the curriculum as a whole.

(*b*) The development, and trial use in schools, of those *methods and materials* which are judged most likely to achieve the objectives which teachers agree upon.

(*c*) The *assessment* of the extent to which the development work has in fact achieved its objectives. This part of the process may also be expected to provoke new thought about the objectives themselves.

(*d*) The final element is therefore *feedback* of all the experience gained, to provide a starting-point for further study.[1]

This last point suggests that curriculum development is a cyclical process and it is indeed helpful to think of it in this way.

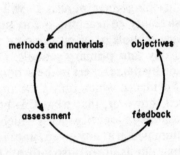

Figure 1.   Curriculum process

Such a concept of curriculum development implies that there is no one starting-point and that it is a never-ending process. For purposes of discussion there has to be a starting-point and a particular sequence of the stages in the process has to be sug-

[1] Schools Council Working Paper No. 10, *Curriculum Development: Teachers' Groups and Centres* (H.M.S.O., 1967).

gested, but in the practical situation this is not necessarily so. This point will be developed fully in a later chapter.

THE NEED FOR PLANNING

Nowadays there is a greater interest in education on the part of the general public and employers. Schools and teachers are frequently criticised for the education they are providing and teachers are being encouraged, or even pressurised to make changes. Most people would accept that there must be innovation of some kind. We live in a changing society in which new knowledge is constantly being discovered and in which old knowledge is being proved wrong. It is no longer possible for even highly educated specialists in some fields to know everything in their own specialism. This problem of the tremendous increase in knowledge means that there has to be an even greater selection of what is to be learned as well as a reconsideration of how learning should take place. With the realisation that pupils must be prepared to cope with the demands of a society which is changing so quickly, teachers need to reappraise what they are offering to their pupils. The fact that a wider range of objectives is being sought in schools emphasises the need for careful planning.

Naturally enough in a changing society, the schools, which are a part of that society, are changing too. The last few years have seen changes of many kinds. There have been changes in the structure of schools, like the development of comprehensive education and the introduction of middle schools. There have been considerable changes in attitudes to discipline and relationships between teachers and pupils. There has been a blurring of subject boundaries, the introduction of a greater variety of teaching methods, the use of a wide range of audio-visual aids and the development of new techniques of examining. These are some of the more prominent changes in recent years. It might be argued, in the light of a vast amount of evidence of change which could easily be amassed, that teachers are doing enough, and that they are in fact responding sufficiently to the demands of a changing society.

THE ELEMENTS OF THE CURRICULUM

Two answers can be given to this argument. The first is that teachers tend to be practical people, very much concerned with getting on with the job of teaching the pupils in the classroom. This attitude has led them to be concerned very largely with only two aspects of curriculum development, namely those connected with content and method. Consequently, changes that have taken place have tended to be concerned with content and method although objectives are implicit in these changes. Important as these two aspects of learning and teaching are, they should not be treated in isolation from the other two aspects of the curriculum, objectives and evaluation. As we shall see later, the four aspects are closely interrelated and changes to any one aspect may affect all the others. This close relationship is illustrated in the following diagram:

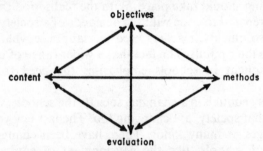

Figure 2.   Elements of the curriculum

The elements in Figure 2 can be compared with the diagrammatic representation of the curriculum process in Figure 1. There is a difference only in terminology: content is used instead of materials, and assessment and feedback have been put together as evaluation. Each element of the curriculum is given thorough study and attention during the process of curriculum development.

A LOGICAL PROCESS

The second answer to the argument that teachers are responding to the demands and need for change is related to the first, and the point has been made previously. It is that change should be planned and introduced on a rational and valid basis according to a logical process, and this has not been the case in the vast majority of the changes that have already taken place.

The reason for this deficiency is quite clear: the knowledge and skills necessary to undertake curriculum development in such a way have not in the past been part of a teacher's initial training. (This situation is currently being remedied in some areas of the country.) It is well known that teachers in this country have always cherished their freedom to decide what they should teach and how they should teach it, a privilege which colleagues in other countries do not always have and which they may regard with a certain envy. However, this privilege brings with it certain responsibilities, including that of providing for pupils an education which is relevant to the society in which they live now and to the kind of society in which they are likely to live as adults. This means that teachers must acquire sufficient knowledge, skill and experience to make the kind of decisions which will enable them to do this. Such expertise and experience is not acquired overnight and there is some evidence[1] that continuing teacher education of this kind might best be achieved through actual participation in curriculum development activities, a setting in which theories are put to the test in a practical situation. This evidence points the way to an alternative form of in-service education for teachers, a form which would have a real influence on classroom practice.

THE PRESENT POSITION

Some teachers have always been interested in and willing to carry out curriculum change, and this is certainly true of present-day teachers. One has only to visit schools of all kinds or even to read educational journals to find evidence of the vast amount of innovation and experimental work which teachers are undertaking at the present time. The question arises, however, whether the innovations and the experimental work are being carried out for sound educational reasons or whether they are the result of some teacher's whim or fancy, or of someone jumping on to an educational bandwagon, or of an educational 'keeping up with the Jones's', or of the work of one or two highly gifted teachers

[1] From the North West Regional Curriculum Development Project.

developing an idea which worked for them and their pupils in their particular situation, but which might not be relevant or suitable for other teachers and pupils in other situations. Reasons such as these are not sufficiently soundly based for making curriculum change and must be replaced by reasons with a more logical and valid basis.

Other teachers might be described as traditionalists; they accept and follow the pattern that has been long established in the school without considering whether it is what ought to be offered to present-day pupils. Other traditionalist teachers offer what they themselves learned at school, in the belief that since it was all right for them it must be all right for their pupils, disregarding the fact that society today is not like the society in which they grew up.

In some cases curriculum content is determined by the interests and abilities of the teachers. Teachers in this country are in a position to inflict their own pet hobbies and interests on their pupils, should they choose to. The deep interests and outstanding abilities of teachers can frequently be used to great advantage in schools, a point which will be developed more fully later, but these sometimes cause an imbalance. Another form of imbalance which occurs in many schools comes about when new subjects are introduced into the time-table or when new sections are introduced into a syllabus. Because there is no properly established and logical basis on which to make decisions about what should be included and what could be omitted and because these decisions are sometimes emotionally based, the time-table and syllabuses become overcrowded and unbalanced.

The need to regard curriculum development as a dynamic and continuing process, which at the same time can serve as a vehicle for continuing teacher education, cannot be stated too strongly. Participation in co-operative curriculum development activities can lead to a greatly increased professionalism in teachers. On the other hand, there may be some danger that with the vast output of schemes from the national curriculum development projects, teachers using these without undertaking any curriculum development work of their own might come to be regarded as technicians rather than professionals.

SETTINGS FOR CURRICULUM DEVELOPMENT

The activity of curriculum development can be carried out in a variety of settings, either by an individual teacher or by groups of teachers working together. An individual teacher can undertake curriculum development for his own class in a primary school or for a subject for one or more classes in a secondary school. Obvious advantages derive, however, from either the whole staff in fairly small schools or groups of teachers in larger schools working together. There is the benefit of their joint knowledge and experience, the benefit of their complementary skills and expertise, the benefit of the ideas that are developed through interaction with each other as well as the benefit of a wider application of the results of their work than would be the case with an individual teacher. Perhaps the greatest advantage that a whole staff or a group of teachers working in their own school have is not only that they can undertake their development work with a detailed knowledge of all the relevant factors about their pupils, themselves, the school and their whole situation but also that there will be a consistency in the curriculum they plan. This point will be discussed more fully later. It will be obvious, however, that within any one school a combination of these approaches could be in operation.

In recent years large numbers of teachers' centres have been established and these provide another setting for curriculum development activities. Work in a teachers' centre has some of the advantages mentioned for groups of teachers working together in their own schools, together with the possibility of expert guidance in the process of curriculum development from the centre leader and the possible provision of resource materials, equipment and facilities which might not be available in all schools. Work in teachers' centres has the advantage of wider interaction than is possible in any one school and the centre provides a setting of a non-hierarchical nature where teachers may discuss new ideas in a situation free from anxiety.

Curriculum development is also carried out at the national level under the auspices of the Schools Council and the Nuffield Foundation. The usual pattern here is for a small team of teachers and lecturers to be appointed to undertake the work on a full-time basis. Materials which they prepare are sent to a small number of schools where they are tried out and commented upon and returned. This procedure may go on several times before the materials are considered suitable for publication. At this stage induction courses are held so that teachers can learn how to use the materials and also how to induct other teachers in their own areas. The materials might be one of two kinds. They could be in the form of programmes, like the Nuffield language courses, where there is a teachers' guide suggesting the methods to be used, and also pupils' materials. Alternatively, they might be more in the nature of resource materials, in which case the teacher would need to incorporate them into a course which he himself would develop.

Large numbers of national projects will be publishing the results of their work during the next few years. In deciding which, if any, of these to use with his pupils a teacher will have a number of decisions to make. There may be two or more courses covering the same area of the curriculum and a choice may have to be made. If nationally published courses state their objectives a teacher must decide if these are compatible with the aims of his school and suitable for his pupils. If the products of a national project are in the form of resource materials the teacher needs to decide if these are suitable for an existing course or whether he can incorporate them into a new course which is compatible with what he is already doing. Such problems of selection, suitability, comparison and compatibility will have to be faced.

The rational approach to a logical process which is being advocated here will help teachers to resolve problems of this kind on the basis of sound and reasoned judgements. It will also enable them, having made their decisions, to incorporate these products more effectively into their own curriculum. Perhaps most important of all, it will enable teachers to undertake soundly based curriculum development work of their own, either individually or with colleagues. Activities such as these play a vital part in making teachers truly professional.

Chapter 2

Curriculum Process: Situation Analysis

Most writers maintain that there are four *major* stages in the process of curriculum development. These are: selection of objectives, selection and organisation of content, selection and organisation of learning experiences (dealt with in this book under the heading of methods) and evaluation. Where these stages are broken down into smaller steps, one of diagnosis is sometimes included and this is usually diagnosis of pupils' attainment, strengths and weaknesses. The viewpoint expressed in this chapter argues for a much wider and more comprehensive approach to diagnosis, an analysis of all the factors which make up the total situation followed by the use of knowledge and insights derived from this analysis in curriculum planning. This viewpoint sees such an analysis as a major stage in the process of curriculum development, which might then be seen as follows:

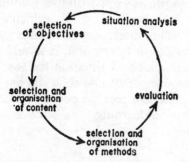

Figure 3. Revised curriculum process

Curriculum development is not an activity which is undertaken once in a school and then is finished. Rather, it is a continuous process, as Working Paper No. 10 suggested, with knowledge and insights derived from assessment being fed back and providing a fresh starting-point for further development. The curriculum itself should be regarded as dynamic rather than static and one of the most important roles of the teacher is to make decisions about a whole range of factors. Each teacher finds himself in a situation which is made up of a number of factors such as pupils, pupils' homes and background, school, its climate, its staff, facilities and equipment. Analysis of these factors, together with a self-analysis, followed by study of their implications for curriculum planning constitutes one step towards the rational approach mentioned in the previous chapter. A situation analysis is most likely to be made at quite a deep level as a preliminary to curriculum planning, again, but less deeply, during development work as a check, again at the point of implementation of the new curriculum (particularly if some of the factors have changed by that time, which might well be the case if curriculum planning has taken a long time), and finally during consideration of the steps to be taken as a consequence of assessment.

In the past much emphasis has been put on teaching, with a corresponding neglect of learning. This may be because acts of teaching are observable and may be judged against some criteria whereas learning itself cannot be seen but only inferred as a result of observing behaviour. Moreover, it is very difficult to assess many kinds of learning. However, more recently increased attention is being given to learning. We have been exhorted for many years now to provide opportunities for pupils to be active participators in learning and while primary teachers have responded well to this exhortation their colleagues in secondary schools have been slower to respond. It should not be thought, however, that in this kind of situation the teacher simply provides materials or equipment and then sits back and waits for learning to take place. His role is a positive and active one; he is there as a facilitator of learning.

THE TEACHER

The teacher usually has the advantage of a course of study and practice to prepare him to carry out his role. He is a person above average in general academic ability, with interests, ideas, abilities and experiences that can be used for the benefit of his pupils. He needs to be able to assess his capabilities without too much over- or underestimation. He needs also to be able to communicate and work with others as well as to be able to develop these skills in his pupils. Since teachers have their strengths and weaknesses, account should be taken of these in curriculum planning. Even in a school where subject specialists are used, the teachers' gifts and talents outside the field of their own particular subjects should be discovered and used. It was mentioned in the previous chapter that one should take care to avoid imbalance in the curriculum and be aware of the dangers of a teacher imposing his particular interests on pupils, but equally, it is often possible to achieve a wide range of objectives which the staff consider desirable by use of the teacher's own talents, interests and hobbies as well as his ability in his particular specialism. Activities of this kind which immediately spring to mind are a school choir or orchestra, a photography club, chess, a teacher's keen interest in travel, rambling, pottery, painting or sport, and there are many more.

As far as weaknesses or deficiencies are concerned, many teachers are prepared to spare no efforts in their attempts to remedy these in the interests of their pupils. They do this by reading, by further study, by consultation with colleagues, by in-service education and by trying out new teaching skills.

In some schools, working in a particularly free way, children and staff all know their own abilities and work together in such a way that sometimes the children are guiding the staff as well as guiding other children. In this kind of learning opportunity, where the greatest possible use is made of everyone's abilities, there is no place for the specialist who sees his subject as sacred and will never venture beyond its confines. This is not an argument against subject specialism nor an argument for integration of subjects; it is merely a statement that in a certain kind of learning opportunity, a free, exploratory one, with pupils and teacher working and learning together, knowledge and skills beyond a particular subject may be required. An explanation ought to be attached to the word 'free'. It is not meant to indicate that the opportunity is aimless, but rather that the particular objectives being pursued require the pupils to investigate, explore or discover, and that there is a broad general framework provided by the teacher within which this is carried on.

It is possible under some circumstances that the teacher may find that his own education hinders as well as helps his function in the school. That which might have been relevant to him as a pupil might not now be relevant for his pupils. He might have attended a college or university where he was encouraged to accept an unimaginative, narrow, subject-based curriculum with an education course in which tutors put forward their own views and ideas without encouraging students to think for themselves. Consequently, when the student becomes a teacher he sometimes finds himself unable to make rational decisions, since he cannot detach himself from school pressures or from his own stereotyped learning and concomitant emotions. He then tends either to accept what is customary in the school or to fall back on his own experience as a pupil at school and teach what he learned and in the way in which he was taught, or he uses a method or approach advocated during his professional training, which may or may not be suitable for his purposes.

The teacher is not only part of the whole situation but to some extent he is the controller of it, or at least of some of it. Unless he can discuss curriculum matters dispassionately and rid himself, if only for a short time, of emotionally controlled thinking, curriculum development will be difficult, since emotions should not guide curriculum decisions. However, this does not mean that a teacher's feelings about curriculum matters should be ignored, but rather discussed dispassionately and given an objective analysis.

Not very many years ago we had in schools a distinct hierarchy of teachers with the head almost like a dictator, albeit a benevolent one, directing the work of the whole school. There are signs that this situation is slowly beginning to change. It is now becoming increasingly accepted that no matter how good the head might be the school cannot function sufficiently well on his ideas alone. The dictatorship that did exist is becoming a democracy, with the head and senior members of staff acting more as co-ordinators and facilitators and with every teacher having a part to play in curriculum planning. Every teacher, even the young and newly qualified, has something to offer to curriculum development and should accept that it is part of his professional responsibility to participate. He should not be willing to leave so much of the thinking and planning to the head or to others outside the school.

When curriculum development is carried out on a group basis it can provide a means of continuing teacher education. Few teachers would assert that when they finish their training they know all that they will ever need to know or that what they are offering to their pupils this year will necessarily be appropriate next year or the following year. Participation in curriculum development work offers a partial solution to both these problems. In undertaking curriculum development teachers become involved in a reappraisal of their work and in doing this further their professional knowledge and gain new insights and expertise. This increase in knowledge, insights and expertise, in turn, can give teachers a feeling for change.

Security will come from knowing how and why change takes place and from having the ability to take part in controlling this change. Security of this kind will replace security which comes from curriculum inertia.

Having carried out an analysis of himself as one of the main elements in the total situation and having decided to take an active and fully professional part in curriculum planning, the teacher then needs to consider other elements or factors.

THE PUPILS

Quite naturally the pupils will be the major factor with which teachers will be concerned and so are likely to be considered first. All teachers know that pupils differ, that some differ greatly and that no two are identical. There are certain general trends and tendencies which may be observed, but basically each pupil is an individual. The matter of individual differences usually receives considerable attention in the theoretical aspect of the professional training of teachers. Some of these differences are apparent and immediately observable by a teacher seeing a class for the first time; these will tend to be physical differences. Others, such as differences in personality and temperament, will make themselves seen after a fairly short period of time. It will take longer for the teacher to become aware of others, but over a period of time it will become obvious that there is a lack of uniformity in what is learned, in the rate of learning, in attitudes towards learning, in the ways of learning. Pupils in a class will also have had a range of different experiences at home or in previous schools, and because of these factors any single learning opportunity which a school is offering will mean something different to different pupils.

All this is well known. Teachers are able to quote examples from their own experience of a wide variety of differences and accept the theory put across during their training that they should take individual differences into account and that they should provide pupils with an education which caters for these differences. This is the theory, but what happens in practice? The very best primary school practice really takes account of differences in pupils and provides for individualised learning. Many primary teachers have moved some way towards the provision of individual learning, but most secondary teachers find this a major problem. It is recognised that examinations have their influence on the curriculum, and many secondary teachers will argue that it is impossible for pupils to be treated as individuals when they are all working towards the same examination. But there is more than one way of reaching the same goal and if pupils really are different in the aspects already mentioned why should they all have to pursue the goal in the same manner? Moreover, it is not uncommon for pupils, even non-examination pupils, to be offered identical learning opportunities—the same content, the same skills, the same way of learning, the same means of expression, the same everything.

It is not only secondary teachers who offer the same educational diet to all. One still hears, if only occasionally, of children being 'expected' to begin reading at about the age of six, which can lead to the position in which four- or five-year-olds are discouraged from reading when they could well do so because of their pre-school experience and ability, or of older children being forced to attempt reading before their past experience has prepared them sufficiently for this learning.

Some teachers consider that streaming or setting is the solution to the problem of individual differences and believe that when pupils are allocated to a form on the basis of general ability or some measure of attainment they can then all be treated in the same way. Frequently pupils in different 'streams' are treated in a very similar fashion; a similar curriculum is offered to all, but some are expected to learn more slowly and to learn less than others. This is not to be taken as an argument against streaming, because the same approach can operate in a school with mixed ability grouping. It is not unknown for pupils in such groups to be treated in exactly the same way with modified expectations as to amount and rate of learning.

The teacher who provides for individual learning is rare and it is fully recognised that it is an extremely difficult thing for teachers to do. However, it is an ideal towards which the profession should be moving, and as the possibilities of the wide range of technological aids become more fully realised and provision of these aids becomes more generous the task should become less difficult.

Pupils exert another kind of influence on the curriculum. Older pupils particularly may indirectly bring about curriculum change because they show little regard for the curriculum being presented. It would be very difficult to know, for example, in connection with recent approaches to the teaching of religious education in the secondary school or with the wide range of courses offered to older non-examination secondary pupils, to what extent these changes were introduced because teachers felt they were more appropriate or because pupils forced them to reconsider the curriculum. It is likely that both factors were operating in some schools.

THE ENVIRONMENT

The environment in which a school is situated and from which it draws its pupils provides another range of factors which the teacher must analyse and take into account in curriculum planning. Two of the greatest environmental influences on the pupil are his family and his peer group. Within the family itself factors such as its size, the pupil's position within it, the relationship between the parents, their attitude to education, their level of aspiration, the absence of one parent, will all have their effect on the child, an effect which may either help or hinder learning, sometimes dependent upon the curriculum being offered. The influence of the peer group on a child is very strong, particularly during the period of adolescence. Teachers need to be very much aware of the relationships that exist in their classes and to assess the effect on learning which they might be having. Sometimes the influence of the peer group may be a hindrance to learning, when, for instance, the level of aspiration and motivation towards learning are low. Sometimes the relationships which exist among pupils in a class can be used to help learning. Friendship groups are often used in primary schools in group work but less frequently in secondary schools. This may be particularly the case in 'difficult' secondary schools where there are feelings of antagonism towards a teacher from pupils, making the teacher reluctant to allow friends to work together in groups for fear of greater antagonism, bad behaviour and little work being done. However, even in such cases, with opportunity to acquire the necessary skills for productive group work and with appropriate selection of learning tasks, antagonism and bad behaviour can be reduced or eliminated and positive attitudes to learning encouraged.

The teacher must understand the influences of both the family and the peer group, indeed the influences of the whole background of the child, and take account of them in curriculum planning, using positive influences to advantage and trying to overcome the negative influences. Knowledge of pupils' background can provide the teacher with a point of contact with his pupils and will suggest many starting-points for new learning. Again, all this is well known to teachers, and while knowledge of pupils' background is frequently used in connection with pastoral care, one suspects that the extent to which it is used in curriculum planning is minimal.

THE SCHOOL BUILDING

The school building and its facilities, equipment and materials are other factors which must be taken into consideration in curriculum planning. It may be that in some cases these will be inhibiting factors, while in others they will offer a variety of opportunities. In either case, the important thing is to consider the building and its facilities and to decide how they can best be used, what are their advantages and disadvantages and what possibilities they offer. Even the oldest and most unattractive buildings have some possibilities and one can see such buildings, old and ugly on the outside, transformed almost miraculously on the inside, with the walls a blaze of colour, odd corners displaying models of all kinds, with examples of the pupils' work making this transformation.

Space is another aspect of these factors which ought to be given serious thought. In old, cramped buildings teachers are often forced into the position of having pupils work in odd corners all over the building, both inside and outside. Why should this practice be restricted to such schools? Surely, there are advantages to be gained in all kinds of schools from making the maximum use of all the available space. Many objectives which teachers consider desirable can be pursued to advantage in this way. This does, of course, involve planning by the whole staff, as does the use of all the available facilities and equipment in the school, and co-operation in carrying out the plans. A school in which pupils work in this way, with individuals and small groups working and displaying their work in spaces all over the building, rather than only in their own classrooms, will give the impression to visitors of allowing a great deal of freedom to its pupils, and while this may be so, it should be realised that in order to give this kind of freedom the staff have been involved in a great deal of planning and have worked in a spirit of co-operation and goodwill, and that the freedom is within a certain structure and has not been achieved overnight.

THE SCHOOL CLIMATE

Finally, the school climate, the sum total of the values and attitudes held by those in the school, the relationships that exist—in fact, everything the school reflects—must be considered. Because of its all-pervading nature the school climate will influence every aspect of the curriculum—choice of objectives, content, materials, methods and evaluation. A school climate usually develops slowly, but may be changed considerably by the appointment of a new head teacher or a large number of new teachers. It is rare for a staff to analyse the climate of the school and this would not be an easy task, especially carried out in isolation. As part of the process of curriculum development, however, and indeed permeating all curriculum planning activities, a reappraisal of many facets of climate would take place. Questions would be asked about what the school was trying to achieve, on what aspects of education it placed greatest value, whether teacher–pupil relationships were of the kind that contributed best to the school's purposes, whether teaching–learning methods were appropriate, and many more besides.

These then are some of the factors which need to be analysed and taken into account in curriculum planning. All are important and their implications must be recognised, but in certain cases and on certain occasions, one factor might have to be given particular emphasis. This would be the case in a school where certain factors were different from 'normal', for example in the case of a school with a high proportion of immigrants or a school in a new town. Teachers will no doubt think of other factors which are of particular importance in their own situation.

The analysis of the situation is directed by what teachers feel may be of practical help. When it has been undertaken they may be expected to have greater knowledge and understanding which they can then use to help the design of their curricula. In this way links can be established between carefully diagnosed situations and what teachers and pupils do.[1] Under these circumstances it is unlikely, for example, that teachers would require identical lock-step activities to achieve common objectives from pupils they had found to be different.

All this is asking a great deal of teachers. We are advocating that a curriculum should be designed for each individual school and modified for each individual pupil within the school, on the grounds that each school is unique and each pupil is unique. Perhaps this is asking the impossible, but nevertheless it is an ideal towards which we should be working, and teachers need to be equipped to do this as part of their professional duties. It has already been mentioned that the acquisition of the knowledge and expertise to do this may well provide teachers with the security that is being swept away in the path of change. In fact, more and more teachers are accepting this kind of challenge and responsibility, and increasing numbers are spending part of their week doing their 'normal' duties and part of the week in curriculum development activities.

Teachers who do this are fully professional. However, there is the possibility that some teachers may be both willing and prepared to accept a curriculum devised by an outside body and to put this into action uncritically and without modification to fit their own objectives and situation. In this case, they may be judged not to be functioning in a creative, responsible and fully professional manner.

Although the task of teaching is becoming a far more difficult and complex one, there are many more aids to help the teacher. In the first place he now has a longer training which ought to

[1] For simple examples to illustrate the linking of factors found in the situation to the designed learning opportunities see Appendices A and B (pp. 107 and 111).

mean that he is better able to cope as a newly qualified teacher. Moreover, many colleges of education are now including curriculum development as part of professional training. There are many more opportunities for the in-service education of teachers, both short-term and long-term. The newly developing teachers' centres are offering in-service education of many different kinds. There is an abundance of educational books and journals for the teacher. Schools themselves have improved in design; generally, there is more money available and books, materials and equipment of high quality can be obtained. Some teachers have ancillary helpers to relieve them of non-professional duties. So the picture is not all black, and although greater demands are being made on teachers, there are many more resources to be called upon.

The important thing for teachers to remember is that we are faced with a living, changing situation and that this requires a changing curriculum. Sometimes the changes will be small, while at other times they might be quite drastic. Part of the teachers' responsibility is to make decisions about the nature and direction of the changes required. Any teacher presenting the same learning opportunities to pupils for two consecutive years must ask himself if he has reappraised the situation. If nothing else is thought to have changed, he himself will be one year older and have one more year's experience.

Chapter 3

Curriculum Process: Objectives

The question 'What should I be trying to get my pupils to achieve?' appears on the surface to be a perfectly straightforward one. Yet it frequently causes some difficulty. It is a question which some teachers never seem to ask themselves. Student teachers in colleges of education about to embark on a teaching practice frequently ask themselves and their tutors, 'What shall I teach?' 'What methods shall I use?' But seldom do they ask, 'What should I be trying to get my pupils to achieve?' It is true that somewhere in their preparation notes there usually appears a brief statement about the aim, but this is frequently expressed in terms of content to be learned or a skill to be acquired. It is not uncommon for trained and experienced teachers, when asked what their objectives for their pupils are, to answer in terms of content and basic skills, giving their answer in such a way as to indicate that they had not really thought deeply about what they were trying to achieve.

There are, of course, other teachers who have thought about objectives and who know what they are hoping to achieve. In some cases, they might be rather vague ideas, somewhere in the back of the teacher's mind, never really expressed in words, but there, nevertheless, guiding everything the teacher is doing with his pupils. In other cases, the objectives may be very clear, openly expressed, known to the pupils, but perhaps rather restricted in range. An example of this might be that of a teacher who states that getting pupils to pass examinations is his sole concern.

There are, it must be admitted, those who argue quite strongly against the whole idea of expressing what they hope to achieve as behavioural objectives. Before reviewing some of their main arguments, it might be useful at this point to explain what is meant by behavioural objectives and to distinguish between these and aims. Education can be described as a process which is intended to bring about certain desirable changes in the behaviour of pupils, that is to say, changes in what pupils think, or the way they act or feel. These changes in behaviour, expressed in the form of what the pupil is expected to be able to do at the end of a course or a series of lessons, are behavioural objectives. For example, we might say that at the end of a short course in simple cookery it is hoped that pupils will be able to:

(1) Make a cheese dish.
(2) Bake bread.
(3) Prepare two kinds of pastry.
(4) Make cakes from a rubbed-in mixture.

These are the objectives expressed in behavioural terms of this particular short course in simple cookery and it is possible to assess whether the pupils have achieved them. This course might be part of a longer and more complex course which has certain aims. Among these might be:

(1) To help the pupils to become good cooks.
(2) To develop in the pupils a love of the creative aspects of cookery.
(3) To help the pupils to understand the scientific basis of cookery.

These aims are much more general than the objectives stated above and serve the purpose of indicating the general direction of the course. (Further points about the differences between aims and objectives will be made later in the chapter.)

ARGUMENTS FOR AND AGAINST THE USE OF BEHAVIOURAL OBJECTIVES

Those who argue against the use of behavioural objectives usually do so on four main grounds, although several additional arguments are frequently brought forward. One argument claims that stating objectives behaviourally leads to an overemphasis on trivial outcomes of learning with a corresponding neglect of important outcomes. While it is true that it is much easier to express what might be called trivial behaviours as operational objectives and that these are frequently given as examples (as in the case above), usually to illustrate a point simply and clearly, it does not necessarily follow because of this that trivial outcomes need be emphasised at the expense of those of greater importance. By stating objectives clearly and explicitly we are in a position to assess the importance of what we are trying to teach and to reject that which is unimportant and trivial. Much that is trivial and unimportant can be taught under the umbrella of a fine-sounding aim: to develop an appreciation of good literature, to help pupils to become good citizens, to develop the ability to discriminate. Aims such as these can lead the teacher to present both trivial and important activities for pupils; an interpretation of what these aims mean in terms of pupil behaviour can lead to a clear distinction between them.

Critics of the use of behavioural objectives also argue that by stating objectives in advance teachers are not able to take advantage of opportunities which occur unexpectedly in the classroom. This is not so; teachers can use these unexpected opportunities and direct them towards objectives which are considered important and desirable. Regarded in this way, unexpected opportunities lead to progress rather than to mere diversion. On the other hand, a teacher with no predetermined objectives might be accused of using such opportunities for entertainment purposes or as a temporary diversion.

The fact that behaviourally expressed objectives lend themselves to assessment brings forth criticism from some quarters, together with another argument that there are other important outcomes of education besides those which can be assessed. The first of these arguments is part of the strong feeling that is sometimes expressed against measurement of all kinds, and yet teachers are constantly making evaluative judgements of their pupils' abilities and performance. To the proponents of the second argument one can only urge patience and experiment; we must either wait for someone else to develop measuring devices for those behaviours that are currently thought to be 'unmeasurable' or, better still, we must try to devise some ourselves.

The difficulty of writing objectives in certain areas of the curriculum causes some critics to reject the whole idea of objectives. It is true that it is very difficult to express objectives in behavioural terms in the arts and the humanities, but this is no reason for not trying. In these areas of the curriculum it is not uncommon to find objectives which begin 'to appreciate . . .' This is a very vague expression with a variety of possible interpretations. An example of an objective expressed in this way will illustrate the kind of difficulties involved. In an English course an objective might be that the pupils will appreciate good literature. What does this mean? How does the teacher know when the pupil is appreciating good literature? What *is* good literature? Is the pupil achieving this objective if he has at home a large collection of books, or if he is a member of the library, or if he is emotionally moved after reading Dickens, or if he can recite the plct of novels read recently in class? Teachers need to decide what they mean by appreciation of literature for the purpose of this particular course and exactly what their pupils will be doing when they are appreciating literature. Only then can they know if their pupils are making progress in the desired direction.

STATEMENT OF OBJECTIVES

The ideal position, in the opinion of the writers of this book, is for teachers to have a fairly wide range of objectives which are clearly and precisely expressed.[1] These objectives can then be used to plan the learning opportunities of the pupils and to devise means of assessing the extent to which the pupils have achieved the objectives. We must, as teachers, have a very clear idea of where we are going in order to have a rational basis to guide and direct the activities in the classroom; equally, we need to know the extent to which our intentions have been successful and this knowledge is provided by the assessment.

This idea of having a clearly set-out statement of what one hopes to achieve before working out how to set about it seems to be such a simple and sensible one and yet it has received little attention from teachers in the past. This is perhaps partly due to something already mentioned, namely that the prime concern of most teachers is to get on with the job of teaching, which is seen largely as being concerned with content and method. It is perhaps also due to the fact that we tend to speak in rather general terms about education and to use words and phrases rather

[1] For further study and for a more detailed discussion of levels of specificity see H. and A. Nicholls, *Creative Teaching* (George Allen and Unwin, 1975), Chapter 2, particularly pp. 20–6.

loosely and this leads us to feel that there is general agreement about the purposes of education, that we all know what we are trying to do, so we do not need to spend time discussing it or writing it down. In fact, when terms are defined and discussion is pursued, agreement is not so widespread.

So much is being demanded of schools, much more than ever before, that everything must be done for a purpose; time is valuable and none of it can be wasted. This demands an overall plan of action and this plan should begin with a statement of what the objectives are. How can we decide what our objectives should be? Where can we look for guidance about what our pupils should be trying to achieve?

SOURCES OF OBJECTIVES

It was suggested in the previous chapter that a teacher should take as complete a survey as is possible of the situation in which he finds himself. From this assessment of his situation will come suggestions about what he should be trying to achieve and also perhaps an indication of factors which might enhance or limit what he can achieve. Central to the situation are the pupils themselves. Diagnosis of their strengths and weaknesses, their abilities and interests, their approach to learning will indicate their needs which will in turn indicate to the teacher many suitable objectives for his pupils to pursue.

A study of the local environment, including the pupils' homes, might give the teacher further ideas for possible objectives. It may be, just as in his study of his pupils, the teacher will find here a wide range of variations which he will have to take into account. Two major ones in this area will be the attitude towards education in the pupils' sub-culture and the level of language development. The attitude towards education might range from one of antagonism, through apathy and toleration, to high regard. Bernstein's work has shown that the use of language is restricted in some families and that this affects children's ability to take full advantage of their school experiences. Factors such as these must be taken into account by teachers. It could be argued that social factors of this kind should not affect the objectives that we set for our pupils and that objectives should be the same for all our pupils, whatever their social handicaps might be. If this argument is accepted, it would be necessary to take into account the social handicaps when the means to the objectives were being planned, so that different pupils would have different learning opportunities. On the other hand, it is possible to support the argument that objectives for pupils with social handicaps might have to be different, at least for a time until the handicaps had been alleviated, just as with a pupil who could not read, one might plan only for a restricted range of objectives until he had learned to read.

The school itself will have an influence on what the teachers in it are able to achieve. The curriculum in action is a controlled interaction between pupils, teachers, time, space, facilities, materials and equipment, content and activities. The physical environment of the school and the facilities, materials and equipment in it, as aspects of this relationship, will have either a limiting or enhancing effect on the objectives teachers set for their pupils, perhaps not an effect of major importance, but one which merits some consideration and which teachers ought to take into account in their curriculum planning. Far more important in its effect will be the climate and the traditions of the school.

The school climate, the sum of the attitudes of the teachers and the attitudes of the pupils and the relationship between them, could well be in practice the greatest single influence on the curriculum. Wrapped up in this will be what the school stands for, what its priorities are, what its standards are, what it considers to be important. None of this might have been written down or even discussed formally by the staff, but the behaviour of the staff really indicates what their objectives are in this case. Tradition is likely to play a very dominant part here. The climate of a school usually develops over a long period of time and its system of values becomes known in the district and tends to be accepted by teachers joining the staff.

Bound up in all this is the teacher's own philosophy of education, the ideas which he has about the priorities education should be concerned with. Perhaps it is a fact that all teachers have not worked out such a philosophy and so tend to accept the values of the school in which they teach. In undertaking curriculum development a school has the opportunity to help young teachers to work out a philosophy of education and to help more experienced teachers to clarify theirs.

RELATIONSHIP BETWEEN AIMS AND OBJECTIVES

It is important that the objectives that teachers set for their pupils in their classroom activities should be consistent with the overall aims of the school, otherwise the aims are never likely to be achieved and some teachers could be working in opposing directions. This stresses the need for the whole staff to decide together what these aims should be and the need for adequate discussion so that different viewpoints might be put and a consensus of opinion arrived at. Once agreement has been reached about the school's aims, the general direction in which all are working, then individual teachers, groups of teachers or a whole staff can consider the objectives for various aspects of the curriculum which are consistent with the general school aims. It might be found, particularly among a large staff, that it is not possible to arrive at a consensus, that the educational philosophies of members of staff are at such variance that complete agreement about what the school should be trying to do for its pupils can not be reached. A headteacher and his staff facing such a situation might feel that a start could be made in those areas where there was agreement.

The discussion of objectives is not a particularly easy task. It requires clarity of thought, care in definition of terms as well as a great deal of patience and goodwill. It will probably be found with a group that has not previously had experience in this that they reach a point of clarification beyond which at that time they are not able to go and at this stage they would be wise to move on to discussion of how they hope to achieve their objectives. They will find that during this step in the process of curriculum development, as they discuss content, materials and method, there will be a further clarification of the objectives, and again, if there is need for still further clarification, this will occur when techniques of assessment are discussed. However difficult the clarification of objectives may prove to be, it is an operation that cannot be neglected, for without a statement of the objectives there is nothing to guide any decisions which have to be made about the curriculum.

Brief mention has already been made of the influence of tradition on the curriculum. So much goes on in our schools because of tradition and it is not easy for someone to step back and look at the whole picture and ask, 'Why are we doing this?' Participation in curriculum development gives the opportunity to do this; it gives the opportunity to consider whether what previous societies demanded of their schools is relevant to our present society. Changes in society together with the knowledge explosion are two important factors which have caused the present curriculum of our schools to be criticised. It is said that schools are not changing quickly enough, that they are not keeping pace with the changing society and that they are not educating pupils to live in that society. A study of society and of the lines along which it might develop should indicate a whole range of objectives which schools might be pursuing.

In this country teachers have always been encouraged to concern themselves with more than the intellectual development of their pupils. They have been encouraged to consider also their physical, social and emotional development. Over a period of time objectives should reflect the concern for these four aspects of pupils' development, but the balance between the four may well vary considerably, according to the teachers' views on what education should be concerned with, the age and ability of the pupils and the needs of particular pupils at any given time.

An important consideration about objectives and learning opportunities is the need to plan learning to achieve more than one objective. This procedure is obviously more efficient and economical in terms of time. The achievement of multiple objectives is likely to occur whether we plan for it or not, and if unplanned it may well be that some of the objectives achieved are ones which we consider undesirable. For example, a teacher might have as an objective knowledge of the causes of the Wars of the Roses, and because either the topic is not of great interest to a particular group of pupils or because it is taught in an uninteresting way, the pupils might develop a great dislike for history, an objective the teacher certainly did not plan nor wish to achieve.

More desirable multiple objectives are likely to be achieved as a result of careful planning of learning opportunities. If the acquisition and understanding of certain information is the teacher's prime objective at a particular time, the learning opportunity planned to achieve this objective can at the same time be used for the achievement of objectives concerned with, say, intellectual or group skills or certain attitudes or values. If, on the other hand, a teacher's main objective at a particular time is his pupils' increased skill in group functioning, he could plan learning opportunities to develop this and at the same time to promote certain emotional and intellectual objectives. Planning of this kind not only provides for a more economical and efficient use of time but is more likely to result in pupil growth towards the planned objectives since opportunities to practise the desired behaviours will occur more frequently and in a wider variety of situations.

At some stage a decision will have to be made about the number of objectives to be attempted. Again it is a question of trying to reach the point of maximum efficiency, and this will be different according to whether one is planning a course, which might last two or more years, a teaching unit which might last for up to a year, or a learning opportunity within a unit. The conflict might lie in the many objectives the teachers may wish to achieve, the number that the course, unit or opportunity is capable of achieving and also the number of objectives that can be kept clearly in the teacher's mind as he is teaching. The last point is very important. If the curriculum is to be really dynamic and if the final decisions are to be made by the teacher in the actual learning opportunities, then he must keep the objectives he is trying to achieve clearly in mind so that these will guide his decisions. They will provide him with a rational basis on which to decide which of the many pupils' responses he should follow up or develop. It is almost impossible to give a desirable number of objectives since factors like those just mentioned must be taken into consideration. A balance should be sought between a number so small as to make the time spent on related learning activities uneconomical and so large as to make their achievement difficult in the time available. Teachers planning courses based on behavioural objectives for the first time might be wise to limit the number of objectives until they have built up some expertise and experience.

It was suggested earlier that objectives should be concerned with all aspects of pupils' development over a period of time. Examples of objectives dealing with these aspects are listed below. It should be pointed out that these are not necessarily being put forward as desirable objectives, although they might well be so for some pupils, but they are presented as examples to illustrate certain points.

EXAMPLE OBJECTIVES

INTELLECTUAL
  1. Name in French articles of common use in the classroom
  2. Write reports of field-study trips
  3. Find information from a variety of sources
  4. Read books for pleasure in their own time

EMOTIONAL
  5. Show increasing sensitivity towards other people
  6. Display increasing understanding of the self

SOCIAL
  7. Work together productively in groups
  8. Join in out-of-school activities

PHYSICAL
  9. Practise good habits of hygiene
  10. Swim at least twenty-five yards

CLASSIFICATION OF OBJECTIVES

There are a number of points about these objectives which merit discussion. The first concerns the categories into which they have been placed. It was mentioned previously that teachers in this country tend to be concerned with the all-round development of their pupils, and that although certain aspects of pupil development might be given priority on occasions according to particular circumstances, over a period of time attention would be given to a wide variety of objectives. An examination of objectives 4, 5, 7 and 9 shows that it is not always possible to make a clear-cut decision about the category in which an objective might be placed. Reading books for pleasure has a strong emotional component as well as an intellectual one and this objective might well have been included in the second category. Showing sensitivity towards other people has a social element. In productive group work there is often a strong emotional factor as well as the use of certain intellectual skills, while the practice of good habits of hygiene is as much a social objective as it is a physical. So that while we recognise that there are, in general terms, these four aspects of pupil development with which we may wish to be concerned, we should realise that these are not clear-cut categories as far as learning and pupil behaviour are concerned.[1]

FORM OF OBJECTIVES

An examination of the form in which the ten example objectives are written will show that they are expressed in a way that tells us what the learner is doing. They do not tell us what the teacher is doing or what the course is intended to do. These objectives might be compared with the aims of the hypothetical cookery course mentioned previously. These are:

(1) To help the pupils to become good cooks.
(2) To develop in the pupils a love of the creative aspects of cookery.
(3) To help the pupils to understand the scientific basis of cookery.

These are the aims of the course; they tell us what it is hoped the course will achieve. Objectives answer the question 'What will the pupils be *doing* at the end of the course, period of study, etc.?' and so they begin with a verb, such as describe, identify, estimate, select, compare, define, gather data, plan, reorganise, forecast, interpret, verify, argue, plot, express, etc. Objectives written in this form provide a very useful guide to the planning of learning opportunities and offer suggestions about how we can assess whether the pupils are displaying the behaviour indicated in the objectives.

If objectives are written in a way which indicates what the course is intended to achieve they do not serve the same usefulness as guides to planning or as a basis for assessment techniques. This is equally true of objectives which indicate what it is intended that the teacher should do, such as the following:

[1] The classification of objectives suggested here is a very basic one. Readers interested in studying other classifications should read: B. S. Bloom *et al.*, *Taxonomy of Educational Objectives, Handbook I: Cognitive Domain* (Longmans, Green & Co., 1956); D. R. Krathwohl *et al.*, *Taxonomy of Educational Objectives, Handbook II: Affective Domain* (Longmans, Green & Co., 1964); S. Nisbet, *Purpose in the Curriculum* (University of London Press, 1968).

(1) To teach the pupils to become good cooks.
(2) To guide the pupils towards a love of the creative aspects of cookery.
(3) To teach the pupils to understand the scientific basis of cookery.

Another important effect of writing objectives in a form which tells us what the pupil is doing when he is achieving the objective is that it puts emphasis on the learning aspect rather than on the teaching aspect. It cannot be assumed that learning is merely the obverse of teaching and many educationists consider that insufficient attention has been given in the past to the learning process.

CLARITY AND PRECISION

A further examination of the way in which the example objectives are written will reveal differences in the degree of clarity and precision. In some cases it is possible to state quite clearly, in a manner unlikely to be misinterpreted, the behaviour one wishes the pupils to display. Of the ten objectives, the last one, swim at least twenty-five yards, is the one least open to a variety of interpretations. In stating this objective the teacher of physical education is saying that he will be satisfied when his pupils can swim this distance, regardless of style, stroke or speed. If he were concerned with style, the stroke used or the time taken he would add certain qualifications to the objective, but as a minimum performance the original objective is what he has set for his pupils. Objectives 1 to 4 and objectives 8 and 9 are expressed with reasonable clarity and precision, but would probably become more precise when matters of assessment were discussed. One might ask, for instance, 'How many articles of common use would the teacher be satisfied with?' 'How many books would a pupil have to read to have achieved objective 4?' 'How many out-of-school activities?' 'Which good habits of hygiene?' 'Will any suffice?' Similar questions might be posed about objectives 2, 3 and 7. Objectives 5 and 6 are expressed somewhat more vaguely. This is not surprising since these are 'emotional objectives'. It is far more difficult to write objectives which deal with attitudes, values and feelings and since some areas of the curriculum are greatly concerned with such objectives, teachers in these areas have to give considerable thought to the formulation of their objectives.

One approach to the formulation of these more difficult objectives is to argue that when expressed in a rather vague and imprecise way, there is a danger that such objectives provide little guidance for planning and assessment purposes and this could result in the intended behaviours not being acquired at all. In this case, it might be better to be satisfied with something a little less ambitious. If we take objective 5 this point can be illustrated: show increasing sensitivity towards other people. This appears to be a highly desirable objective and one which many teachers might wish their pupils to achieve. But what do we really mean by 'sensitivity towards other people'? Different teachers are likely to interpret this in different ways according to the age, needs and backgrounds of their pupils. The teachers undertaking curriculum planning and including this particular objective would be wise to indicate what *their* interpretation of 'sensitivity towards other people' is in terms of the course they are planning. This objective, developed in this way, might then read as follows—pupils will show increasing sensitivity towards other people so that they:

(a) Listen to the opinions of others in their group.
(b) Help members of their group to carry out tasks.
(c) Take part in community service activities.
(d) Criticise social practices which show lack of consideration for individuals.
(e) Propose alternative practices to those in (d) above.

These five aspects of increasing sensitivity provide clear guidance for the planning of learning opportunities and it would be possible to devise means of assessing pupil growth in each of them. Later, when it was found that the pupils had achieved these objectives to the satisfaction of their teachers, objectives dealing with other aspects of sensitivity to other people could be formulated and learning opportunities planned for the pupils to achieve these. In this way, over a period of time, many aspects of sensitivity could be displayed by the pupils. Objective 6 could be treated in a similar fashion.

An alternative approach to the problem of complex objectives such as these is to direct teaching and learning towards the general statement and to regard the sub-statements as samples of specific behaviours. These will be used later for assessment purposes as evidence of growth towards the objective. In the case of objective 5, teaching and learning would be directed towards the general statement that 'Pupils will show increasing sensitivity towards other people'. The five sub-statements above would be used to assess progress towards the main objective.

Both these approaches provide for increased development towards the objectives and for pupils to make individual progress.

SHORT-TERM AND LONG-TERM OBJECTIVES

It will be obvious that some of the example objectives on page 41 could be achieved in a fairly short period of time, at least by some pupils, while others could be very long-term objectives, even covering the whole of the period of education. Objective 1, name in French articles of common use in the classroom, and objective 10, swim at least twenty-five yards, are shorter-term examples, but these are likely to be less common, particularly at the secondary stage of education. Most objectives are not really points which pupils reach but rather lines along which they are moving. One would certainly expect evidence of movement, in the form of measurable progress, but most objectives would give opportunity for greater refinement of the behaviour implied in the objective, a better performance of whatever the pupil was doing. Even in the case of short-term objectives this is true up to a point. One could look for a better style or a variety of strokes in swimming, or more complex and thoughtful field-study reports, or a wider range of classroom articles or better pronunciation in French. But it is more particularly true of the long-term objectives. The kind of sensitivity towards other people shown by six-year-olds would be different from that which one would expect from sixteen-year-olds. The nature of group work done by nine-year-olds is likely to be less complex than that of fifteen-year-olds.

SPECIFIC AND GENERAL OBJECTIVES

Another difference that might be seen among the ten objectives is that some, such as numbers 1, 2, 4 and 10, are related to a particular area of the curriculum, and these might be called specific objectives, whereas the others are not related to any subject area at all and might be called school-wide or general objectives. The latter would perhaps have been agreed by the whole staff of a school and as the pupils moved up the school the teachers would look for a higher standard of performance in these objectives. In the case of most primary schools where teachers usually have the same class for the whole of the year there is not such a great danger that the general objectives will be overlooked. The junior school teacher will, for example, encourage his pupils to join in out-of-school activities, will provide his pupils with opportunities for learning the skills of seeking information from a variety of sources and will try to develop in his pupils greater sensitivity to other people. Even here, however, there is the need for all this to be continued in successive years in the school so that the pupils achieve a higher performance.

The dangers in the secondary school are greater, because here teachers are generally regarded as subject specialists and the influence of external examinations is very much felt. Responsibility for encouraging pupils to participate in out-of-school activities might be left to the form teacher during the twenty minutes or so he has each day for registration and other form-room business. Teaching pupils to find information from various sources might be considered to be the responsibility of the English teacher, even though the skill would be used in many subjects. The development of greater sensitivity to other people might be left to the Social Studies teacher or perhaps only considered to be important for the early-leaving pupils, who are not restricted by the demands of public examinations. However, if these objectives have been accepted by the staff as desirable ones, then they become the responsibility of all the teachers in the school for achievement by all the pupils. The staff should then provide opportunities for the behaviour implied in the objective to be learned and practised.

Reference was made earlier to the interrelationships between all the aspects of curriculum development: objectives, content, methods and evaluation, and this point cannot be emphasised enough. Many of us have perhaps been guilty of planning a course of work for our pupils and have started by stating our objectives and we might even have written these down at the top of the page. Having done this, however, we have then proceeded to plan the content, materials and methods we intended to use without further reference to the objectives. The objectives are there to guide the selection of content, materials and methods and must be referred to constantly when decisions about these are being made. Ways in which this might be done will be discussed in the next chapters.

Chapter 4

Curriculum Process: Content

In teaching one must teach something to someone, the someone being the pupil and the something the content. Content might be described as the knowledge, skills, attitudes and values to be learned. In the vast majority of schools the curriculum is organised on a subject basis, but teachers may hold different views about the value of subject-matter. Some may believe that it has intrinsic value and should be learned for its own sake, others may believe that it should be taught for use (in other words, that its value depends on the use that is made of it), while others may regard it merely as a vehicle for the development of intellectual abilities, skills, values and attitudes.

Recently much attention has been given to a study of the structure of the disciplines and the possible implications of structure for the teaching and learning of school subjects. Bruner,[1] one of the most influential writers in this field, refers to structure as the principles, organisation and methods of discovery of the subject-matter that makes up the discipline, in other words, the way the discipline is put together. Bruner argues that even young children can be taught the structure of a subject, and he believes that once a pupil can see the relationship of things in a subject, he can put new things into their proper relationships. If Bruner's arguments are valid, the identification of the structure of disciplines and the development of courses incorporating structure in forms which are appropriate for pupils might provide an answer to the problem of the explosion of knowledge. In view of the rapid and constant changes in subject-matter, citizens today need to know how to interpret and evaluate new knowledge.

[1] J. S. Bruner, *The Process of Education* (Harvard University Press, 1960).

However, there appear to be problems with this approach. Where courses have been developed in this way in the United States some otherwise able pupils do not seem able to handle them for reasons not yet known. Moreover, there is no common agreement among scholars about what the structure of any particular discipline is.

Some people, of course, argue against the idea of separate disciplines and for the idea of unity of knowledge. Their approach to the selection of content would be to draw on subject-matter on the basis of problems, themes or topics, thus cutting across traditional subjects in the hope of achieving some kind of unity, frequently termed integration.

An important consideration about content is its close relationship with method. It is often difficult to say exactly where one begins and the other ends.[1] The methods used often have as much influence on what the pupils learn as does the content. For instance, in trying to change pupils' attitudes teachers might find group discussion techniques more successful than direct class teaching. Unfortunately in the planning of courses in the past attention has often been given to content and method without real regard to what it was hoped the pupils would achieve. For instance, questions about integration of content or a subject-based approach might well be resolved by the objectives of a course (or of the school) rather than by a consideration of the intrinsic value of either approach. Where content and method take precedence or are considered in isolation undesirable results may follow. The desired learning may not take place because of lack of real relationship between objectives, content and methods. In place of the desired outcomes, a variety of unplanned and unwanted learnings may occur. If objectives are stated first, and if they are stated clearly and are based on appropriate considerations, they offer considerable guidance in the selection of appropriate content and methods.

There are, however, other factors to be taken into account, and while fully recognising and emphasising the relationship between content and methods, it is proposed to discuss these separately in order to give full consideration to those aspects of each which need to be studied. Before going on to discuss some of these factors there is an important point to be made about the

[1] See H. and A. Nicholls (*op. cit.*) pp. 54–5 for a discussion of the use of the word 'approach'.

overall curriculum pattern of the school and its effect on courses or units developed within it.

When decisions are made first about the curriculum plan for the whole school, for example that it is to be on a subject basis, and that the scope of the curriculum is to be a coverage of facts, then this imposes certain limitations on any development work. It does not prevent further development but it does mean that the teacher undertaking curriculum development is not as free to try out different forms of content organisation. It is recognised that the pressures are very great for schools to adopt a subject-based curriculum, particularly in secondary schools, and no argument to adopt anything different is being presented here. The present form of the subject curriculum tends to be associated with coverage of facts and what teachers may wish to consider is whether this kind of subject curriculum can lead to the kind of objectives they wish their pupils to achieve. Would such a form of subject curriculum lead to the achievement of objectives concerned, for example, with higher mental processes? Or is it the case that so much time is spent by pupils in learning facts that there is little or no opportunity for them to think critically, solve problems, make judgements or analyses? The other point has already been made, namely, that any decision about the overall curriculum pattern has its implications for the planning of courses and units within it.

Whatever view is taken of the overall curriculum pattern and whatever view may be taken of content, it is usually acknowledged that there is far more to be learned than is possible during the period of school education and so some kind of selection has to be made. It is not uncommon, where this is not prescribed by an examining board, for the selection to be made either on the basis of the pupils' or the teacher's interest, or because the teacher feels that a certain piece of knowledge is necessary for the pupils' education. Content is sometimes selected because it is necessary to the understanding of something else or because it might come in useful later. The selection of content tends to be a somewhat haphazard procedure and it also tends to be biased in one way or another. Certain factors can be taken into account to make this less so.

First, it should be remembered that there is a whole range of content which could serve the same objectives. In the example objectives considered in an earlier chapter we can see how this is so. Ability to work productively in groups can be fostered through the use of a wide variety of different content. Reading books for pleasure can be encouraged through a wide range of books. Many of the other example objectives also illustrate this point. This allows for choice, variety and flexibility, and permits considerations other than the objectives also to be taken into account. From this range of content which is available a selection has to be made and it is suggested that the selection is made on the basis of certain criteria, some of which might be considered more important than others. Before content is included in a course it should satisfy these criteria.

CRITERION OF VALIDITY

It is important that content should meet the criterion of *validity*. Content is valid when it is authentic or true. At a time of rapidly increasing knowledge subject-matter used in school can quickly become obsolete. It may be facts which are obsolete but it might also be concepts, principles or theories. This problem exists at many levels in schools. Recently there has been considerable publicity about the fairly widespread use in primary schools of textbooks which contain content which is no longer true. There have been reports of Physics students going on to university who have been taught theories which no longer hold good. Teachers in all kinds of schools need to be aware of this problem and to exercise the greatest caution in the choice of content. The problem also suggests the need for subject teachers to keep abreast of changes in their particular fields.

There is another aspect of validity, which applies to method as well as to content. This is that the content (or method) is valid if it is possible for the objectives to be achieved through its use. For example, if an objective is concerned with the concept of the relationship between man's way of life and his environment, and the content chosen for the achievement of this objective does not show this relationship in a form which can be perceived by the pupils, it does not satisfy the criterion of validity.

CRITERION OF SIGNIFICANCE

Another important consideration in the selection of content is that of *significance*. Schools have frequently been concerned that pupils should learn large bodies of facts. Yet facts are the least significant or meaningful aspects of school subjects and are only important as they contribute to basic ideas, concepts and principles of subjects. If study were to be based on a number of carefully selected principles, concepts or ideas, facts would be learned to illustrate these and would be included only in so far as they contributed to an understanding of these. This would reduce the problem of learning the large bodies of facts which seems to be the bugbear of so many courses at the secondary level.

This is linked with the matter of breadth and depth in the curriculum. Breadth and depth should be appropriately balanced and yet breadth of coverage and depth of understanding appear to be conflicting objectives. If there is too much emphasis on coverage there is likely to be insufficient attention and time given to the development of intellectual skills and processes which organise knowledge and make it useful to the learner or to the development of feelings and attitudes. The suggestion made above, that a number of carefully selected basic ideas, concepts and principles should form the basis of study, with sufficient time for these to be fully understood, so that they might be related to each other and applied to new situations, might result in an appropriate balance between breadth of coverage and depth of understanding.

CRITERION OF INTEREST

Pupil *interest* is an important criterion in the selection of content, but it is one which is frequently misunderstood and taken to excess. To devise a curriculum solely on the basis of pupils' interests, as is sometimes the case in primary schools or with non-academic pupils in secondary schools, is likely to be found restricting. On the other hand to ignore pupils' interests is to lose a strong motivational force and to run the risk of little or no learning taking place. It is necessary to apply this criterion with caution. The range of pupils' interests is limited and the interests are frequently of a transitory nature. Two approaches to this problem would seem to suggest a well-balanced view. The first would be to include nothing in the curriculum *only* because it is of interest to the pupils, but where other criteria may also be satisfied, to use content which can be as closely related as possible to their interests. The second approach might be to give pupils' interests priority when new learning is being introduced, in order to form an immediate link between the pupils and the curriculum

Lest such an application of this criterion should appear restrictive to some teachers it is perhaps worth bearing in mind that pupils' interests can be widened and enriched through the curriculum, so that under favourable conditions this criterion will become less limiting.

CRITERION OF LEARNABILITY

It perhaps seems obvious to say that what is included in the curriculum should be learnable by the pupils, but the criterion of *learnability*, however obvious it may be, is not always satisfied. The main problem is that of adjustment to the abilities of the pupils. Content must be available in forms which are appropriate to the pupils, and these will, of course, be different for different pupils. It is also important that what is to be learned makes a connection with something which the pupils have already learned, and again this will vary from one pupil to another. This suggests the need for variety in the ways in which content is made available and in the manner in which pupils are expected to learn it.

These criteria—validity, significance, interest and learnability —are suggested for application to content before it is included in the curriculum. Ideally, content selected should satisfy all the criteria; certainly no one criterion should be applied in isolation nor carried to an extreme, although under some circumstances some criteria may carry more weight than others.

In many schools, particularly secondary schools, content is seen as the most important element in the curriculum. It is undoubtedly true that what is taught is very important, but if undue attention is given to content teachers may find themselves disappointed that some objectives they consider important have not been achieved by their pupils. Content must be considered in relation to the objectives teachers have set and in relation to the methods to be used for the achievement of the objectives. These three elements, together with evaluation, constitute the curriculum.

Another distinction which is sometimes made is that between a child-centred curriculum and a subject-centred curriculum, the former tending to be associated with primary schools and the latter with secondary schools. Frequently the so-called child-centred curriculum is held to be more desirable or better in some way than the subject-centred curriculum. If the child-centred curriculum means that the child chooses what he wants to do and how he wants to do it and only those things which are of interest to him are included in the curriculum, the outcomes of such a curriculum are likely to be disappointing, to say the least. If the subject-centred curriculum means that content is selected without any reference to the needs, interests, abilities or other characteristics of the pupils, again the results of such a curriculum will be highly disappointing.

In practice, neither extreme is likely to operate and both child and subject are likely to be given appropriate consideration. Even in a subject-based curriculum all the relevant characteristics of pupils should be taken into account, first in the selection of objectives and later in the selection and organisation of content and methods of learning. If such an approach to a subject-based curriculum were adopted the distinction between a child- and subject-centred curriculum would not exist.

Schools and teachers are subjected to many criticisms and pressures and this is to be expected since the school is one of society's important agencies for socialisation. Many of these criticisms and pressures are related to what is taught, the content; teachers are urged to include all kinds of topics in the curriculum, such as driving a car, anti-drug and anti-smoking information, road safety and sex education. They are sometimes criticised for requiring pupils to learn large bodies of facts which do not seem to serve any useful purpose. A further criticism made by pupils and teachers themselves is that new subjects or new aspects of subjects are introduced but nothing ever seems to be taken out and the problem of coverage becomes an enormous one. There never seems to be enough time in the year to cover everything planned. Where there are no clearly understood criteria for the selection of content it is very difficult to resist pressures for additions or to know whether the pressures should be resisted, and it is also difficult to decide what might be omitted. It is likely that some kind of justification could be offered for everything included in the curriculum. But the question is whether the justification has a rational basis. It is suggested that the procedure just outlined for the selection of content, guidance from the objectives followed by the application of certain criteria, provides such a rational basis. By using this approach not only are teachers able to make more rational decisions but are able to justify or defend these decisions against their questioners or critics.

Chapter 5

Curriculum Process: Methods

It was stated in the previous chapter that it is very difficult to separate content from methods and to say where one ends and the other begins. For instance, if pupils are discussing some pictures, the pictures and what the pupils and teacher say or ask about them can be regarded as the content, while discussion might be regarded as the method aspect, although the two are very closely intertwined. Content and methods come together with the pupils and the teacher in a learning opportunity, which might be described as a planned and controlled relationship between pupils, teacher, materials, equipment and the environment in which it is hoped that desired learning will take place. The method aspect of the learning opportunity involves the relationships between pupils, teacher and materials, the organisation of the content, its manner of presentation to pupils and the activities the pupils and teacher carry out.

One of the great difficulties for teachers is that no two children in a learning opportunity will have the same learning *experience*. Even in direct class teaching with the teacher talking to the pupils, some will hear different things, some will understand different things about what they hear, some will remember different things. Each child brings something different to the learning opportunity and sees it in a different way, and the task of the teacher is to structure the pupils' possible experiences in such a way that they will progress towards the desired objectives. An infant coming to school for the first time from a home which has no books may initially require different learning experiences from a child who has had plenty of books at home. A pupil from a family deserted by the father may take a different view of a study of home and family life and personal relationships. For different pupils this might mean variations in content, stimulus materials, methods, ways of expression or in any other aspect of the learning opportunity the teacher considers appropriate. It is only when the teacher examines the output of learning, what the pupil says, writes, makes or what he does, that he can assess what the pupil has in fact learned.

Methods, perhaps, receive more attention than any other element in the curriculum. Study of methods features prominently in initial and in-service teacher education. Books are written about them and articles appear in the educational press. In spite of this attention there appear to be some misunderstandings about methods and their place and function in the total curriculum. Perhaps because of the attention given to it in teacher training, many teachers, particularly in primary schools, consider it to be the most important element in the curriculum. This attitude is encouraged by some people who come into the classroom and make observations on the methods being used. It is true that methods are probably the most obvious part of the curriculum when one goes into a school, but they should not be judged in isolation; their worth lies in the extent to which they facilitate the achievement of the objectives.

Another common belief about methods is that one particular method is the 'best' or 'right' one. Some teachers may claim to 'believe in' activity methods, discovery methods, formal methods, informal methods or progressive methods, whatever these terms might mean, and present an enthusiastic view of one of these. Here again method is being considered in isolation and is regarded as having value in itself and not in relation to a set of desired objectives. It might be the case that certain kinds of objectives can best be achieved through the use of certain methods, but there remains a great deal of experiment and study to be carried out in this particular field. It is probably also the case that certain kinds of objectives such as those concerned with the development of values, attitudes, appreciations and sensitivities are more dependent on the methods used than on the content. But this is a long way from the position that there is a best or right method. The objectives influence the methods, the content influences the methods and the teacher, pupils, school facilities and environment all influence the choice of methods.

Since we still do not fully understand which methods are best suited to particular objectives, what we are doing in selecting one or more methods for use is putting forward a hypothesis to be tested and only at the evaluation stage may we know if the hypothesis holds good. In some cases research findings may give some indication of potentially fruitful methods.

There is also a tendency on the part of some teachers to think that certain methods are 'best' for certain kinds of pupils and this sometimes results in some indirect and somewhat freer methods being used with less able pupils. Such methods might be quite appropriate for some less able pupils under certain circumstances, but they might be equally appropriate for some brighter or more able pupils.

Just as a set of objectives might be achieved through different content, so might different methods serve the same objectives. Again, this provides the opportunity for both teacher and pupils to achieve variety, flexibility and choice. Moreover, a statement of objectives which includes different types of objectives is likely to require a variety of methods for its achievement. Not only does this variety add interest for the pupils and the teacher, but, and this is of far greater importance, it increases the possibilities of learning for the pupils, since all pupils do not learn best *via* the same methods.

ROLE OF THE TEACHER

Change and variety, however, may bring problems for some teachers, particularly where methods are being tried out for the first time. One of these is the problem of understanding the changing role of the teacher in relation to different methods. For instance, if a teacher has been accustomed to the state of affairs in which class teaching has been the main approach, then he has been in a central position, making an exposition of the content, directing, leading and controlling most if not all of what goes on in the classroom. If, in order to achieve objectives concerned, say, with the learning of certain concepts, with ability to study independently and with ability to work productively with others, the teacher plans learning opportunities in which pupils have to work individually, seeking out knowledge on their own, join with others to plan and carry out a task and where discovery methods of learning are used, the role of the teacher here is very different. He is no longer central in the sense that he is the focal point. In contrast with the first learning opportunity described, he no longer comes directly between the pupil and that which is to be learned; he is not the interpreter, director or total controller. Instead, he might act variously as an adviser, a consultant, a questioner, a sounding board for plans and ideas or a guide. He will be relating frequently to individuals and groups, and perhaps only occasionally to the whole class.

PREPARATION

The problem of preparation for different methods sometimes causes difficulty. The nature of preparation varies considerably according to methods used as does the time when it has to be carried out. This point can be illustrated by reference to the two positions just outlined. In the first, preparation would most likely be carried out in advance of the learning opportunity and might consist of selection of extracts from textbooks, provision of a hand-out, selection of pictures, a film or a filmstrip, together with decisions about what the teacher and pupils would actually do, for example, talk, read, write, watch, answer or ask questions and so on. In the second position much of the preparation is also likely to have been undertaken beforehand and it will probably consist of the provision or checking on the availability of a wide range of resource materials, such as text and reference books, filmstrips, tapes, pictures and so on, and also materials from which the concepts to be learned might be discovered. Decisions about what the pupils are to do cannot be made, except in the broadest of terms, because of pupils' greater control in this type of situation, but the teacher's responsibility is to organise and structure the learning opportunities in such a way that the desired learnings can take place. Some further preparation is likely to take place during the activities as pupils' requirements for independent and group work become known, and then again afterwards in readiness for the next opportunity when further requirements have become apparent. Preparation may vary also in that it might, on different occasions, concern the whole class, groups within the class or individual pupils.

RECORD KEEPING

Record keeping becomes rather more difficult in those learning opportunities where there is a variety of methods operating, where there is greater flexibility and greater individualisation of learning. The importance of careful record keeping cannot be overemphasised. It is essential to the evaluation of pupils' progress towards the desired objectives and it provides valuable evidence on which to base future curriculum decisions. Learning opportunities such as the one described above in which the teacher is removed from the central directing position do offer advantages in relation to the keeping of records. The teacher is more free to observe individuals and is more likely to be in a position to know the pupils well and to assess more accurately what progress is being made.

GROUPING

In addition to the kind of problems just outlined the use of different methods has other implications. One of these concerns different forms of grouping. In the pursuit of different objectives, methods which require various forms of grouping may suggest themselves. Size may be one factor in this variety: for different purposes groups may range in size from two members to the number in the whole class. The manner and basis for forming groups may vary according to the objectives desired: there might, on appropriate occasions, be complete free choice, or formation might be on a restricted friendship basis, e.g. at least two friends in the same group, or on a complementary skills basis, or mixed or similar ability basis or on a sex basis. Most groups will tend to be formed horizontally, i.e. containing pupils from the same class or year group, but vertical grouping might best serve some objectives. Some primary schools are completely organised in this way, while examples in secondary schools would include school journeys and school clubs and societies. Another variation in grouping might be its stationary or flexible nature. For some purposes, a group having been formed needs to stay together until the purpose has been achieved, for example, the task completed, the model made, the discussion ended. For other purposes, a flexible arrangement, with pupils moving from one group to another and with groups changing their size and basis for composition, might be more appropriate. For instance, a group might wish to call upon the services of a member of the class who has a particular talent, or on several members to help in a task which is too great for them, while members of the group might on occasions help other groups in similar ways. The important point to bear in mind with these variations, is not that any one of these has any virtues *per se* over the others, but for some purposes some might be considered more appropriate and it is worth trying them out to find out whether this is in fact the case.

PUPIL–TEACHER RELATIONSHIPS

The choice of a particular method has implications for a range of factors related to pupil–teacher relationships. One of these has been touched on briefly during the discussion of teacher role. Relationships between teacher and pupil will vary according to whether pupils are working individually or in groups or in a class. They will vary also according to the amount of direction the teacher gives. In a learning opportunity controlled and directed by the teacher he may appear as a figure of considerable authority, perhaps as the fount of all knowledge, whose wisdom is not to be questioned. In a more flexible arrangement, such as the one described earlier, he may appear as a figure with whom pupils may discuss their work, who may offer suggestions without always expecting them to be accepted, who encourages inquiry and questioning and who sometimes admits there is something he does not know and is prepared to learn alongside his pupils and from his pupils, recognising that learning is a two-way process. In such a case the teacher is willing to give pupils greater responsibility for their own learning, to allow them to exercise judgement and to make some choices in relation to their learning. This does not mean, of course, that the teacher is abdicating his responsibility; far from it, because, as has been indicated, he has a very positive role to play. Nor does it mean that his authority is any the less. The teacher will always retain the final authority, but it does mean that his authority is less obvious and obtrusive.

ORGANISATION

Another implication of using a variety of methods is related to certain aspects of organisation. Good and efficient organisation is always important in schools and classrooms but its nature may change according to the approach being used. In learning opportunities where there is considerable use of materials and equipment and various groupings, pupils particularly need to know what are their responsibilities and restrictions and what procedures are to be adopted. It may be, of course, that teacher and pupils reach these decisions together. It must be expected that some methods will require a rearrangement of classroom furniture. This might seem to be a small point, but the arrangement of desks can have considerable effect. Consider a classroom with desks arranged in rows. Pupils at the front speaking to the teacher at the front might not be heard by those at the back, who in any case can only see the back of their heads. In order to see someone speaking from the back pupils at the front need to turn round. This kind of arrangement does not help pupil interactions.

Certain methods will require and result in greater movement about the classroom and also in an increase in noise level. This sometimes worries teachers trying out methods for the first time, because they consider it to be a sign of loss of control on their part and they are concerned about what the head or their colleagues might think. It may in fact signify a change in the form of control, but this is a deliberate choice on the part of the teacher, in the hope that certain desired objectives might best be achieved in a less teacher-dominated learning opportunity. The worry and concern would be proper if the noise were so great as to disturb others and interfere with their work.

The teacher, of course, is an important element in any learning opportunity and it was suggested in an earlier chapter that the teacher would find it helpful to make an analysis of himself, of his strengths and weaknesses. It could be that some of his weaknesses are in his ability to use certain methods, or it might be that certain personality or temperament factors cause him to avoid the use of certain methods. Even when all other factors indicate that a particular method might be the most effective in a given learning opportunity, a teacher may decide that, for personal reasons, he could not cope with it and would go on to choose a different method. Another teacher, however, in a similar position might decide to seek the guidance, support or advice of a colleague whom he knows to be skilled in the use of the particular method so that he might become more competent in its use. Such a decision can only be made by the individual in the light of all the factors under consideration.

It has already been suggested that all pupils do not learn best through the same method and that the ideal towards which we should be striving is for a curriculum which is modified for each pupil. It might be decided, in planning a course, that there is a basic minimum of required learning for all pupils and after this has been achieved pupils might make progress towards other additional individual objectives. This whole question of individual differences and the subsequent need to provide for these in the curriculum is proving to be a difficult problem for many teachers. The evidence that pupils are different and learn differently is there to be seen and this is accepted. It is the act of translating this knowledge into the curriculum and making provision for individual differences wherein the difficulty lies. Streaming, grouping or setting are sometimes seen as an answer to the problem, but even within a group or set differences may be great. It is not only a question of variations in ability and interests, but also in ways of learning, preferred media for learning and preferred ways of expression.

This is why it is so important that within any learning opportunity a variety of approaches should be made available. It is particularly important when new knowledge or ideas are being presented; the presentation should be made in a variety of ways, using different media so that each pupil's initial encounter with the new knowledge or ideas has meaning for him. Opportunities to consolidate the learning through other media or in other ways should be available, so that the pupil's range is extended. Similarly with expression of learning or ideas; pupils will prefer certain ways of expression, find some easier than others and the curriculum should make provision for these and also for the pupil to extend his range. For all pupils, a learning opportunity should provide a balance of activities that represent intake of ideas, reflection or the application of intellectual skills on the ideas and expression of learning related to the ideas. Too often learning opportunities are heavily loaded with intake activities and little provision is made for thinking and expression of learning.

There is no escape from the fact that it is not easy either to devise a curriculum which makes this kind of provision or to implement it. The demands it makes on the skill, insights, knowledge, patience and strength of the teacher are very great indeed.

However, more and more aids of all kinds are becoming available to teachers to help them in their task and teachers need to become aware of the kinds of use to which these might be put. Such aids would include many that are in common use already such as books, pictures, filmstrips, slides, films, records, tapes, radio and television broadcasts and resource materials of all kinds. What might be less common is the way in which these are used. Individual pupils or small groups might use particular aids for a particular purpose, sometimes on their own without the teacher. Even quite young children are sufficiently responsible and competent in the use of machines these days, being accustomed to using quite sophisticated equipment such as television sets, tape recorders, washing-machines and automatic sewing-machines at home.

At the beginning of this chapter it was stated that method is one aspect of a learning opportunity which is planned for the achievement of desired learning. In order to make the most efficient use of time available learning opportunities should be planned in such a way as to provide for the pupils' progress towards a number of objectives. This would mean, for instance, that while pupils are acquiring certain knowledge they might also be developing certain skills or attitudes. The methods selected to promote learning should ensure that while catering for one aspect of learning another aspect is not inhibited. Some teachers, for example, put considerable emphasis on the happiness of their pupils. Care should be taken, however, that in seeking to make pupils happy, other important objectives are not neglected or even inhibited. For example, where pupils take part in community service activities which they enjoy, care should be taken to provide opportunities for pupils to progress towards appropriate objectives such as those concerned with the development of social responsibility and social awareness. Too often, community service activities are seen as an end in themselves or it is assumed that there will automatically be progress towards certain social objectives as a result of participation in them. It is more likely that the use which is made of the experiences pupils have in these activities will determine the nature and extent of progress towards objectives. Similarly, in a primary school where pupils have considerable choice in and control over their activities, they are likely to be happy and enjoy working in this way, but teachers should take care that they make appropriate progress in reading and number work, for example.

ORGANISATION OF LEARNING OPPORTUNITIES

Organising a learning opportunity so that the desired learning takes place is one of the crucial tasks in curriculum development. The attainment of objectives usually takes a long time. A single learning experience which a pupil has may have very little effect on him, so that the problem is to arrange learning opportunities in such a way that they support and reinforce each other. In order to do this, learning opportunities must be related in certain ways. For example, what is learned in Geography in the first year may be related to what is learned in the second year and this is described as a vertical relationship. Similarly, what is learned in Geography in the first year may be related in some appropriate ways to what is learned in History during the same year, and this is referred to as a horizontal relationship. If first- and second-year Geography are related in this way the chances are increased of building on what is learned and so leading to greater progress towards the desired objectives. If first-year Geography and first-year History are related appropriately, and this need not be only in terms of content, this may lead to a more unified view of learning by pupils and desired learnings might be reinforced; if they are not related, experiences in one might be in conflict with those in the other, and pupils may also come to regard learning as being in compartments.

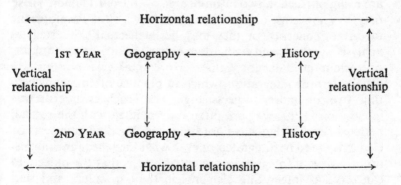

Figure 4.   Vertical and horizontal relationships in learning

In the case of vertical relationships the methods used in a learning opportunity must make provision for pupils to learn the behaviour indicated in the objectives. If, for instance, an objective is concerned with the ability to find information about apple crop production from a variety of sources, frequent opportunities must be made available for pupils to learn how to do this. The number of opportunities needed by particular pupils will vary as will the particular skills at which different pupils are already competent. Pupils may need, for example, to learn how to use an index, or a table of contents, or a set of encyclopedias or a library catalogue.

As well as this aspect of vertical relationships there is another to be taken into account. Over a period of time it is not sufficient that opportunities should be provided which demand behaviour at the same level of difficulty or complexity. Rather one opportunity builds on the level of performance displayed in the previous one. In the case of finding information about crop production from a variety of sources in the example just quoted, this might mean a wider variety of sources, more difficult or complex sources and information of greater depth (see Figure 5). This kind of provision is often well taken care of by teachers in classes they are teaching, and in successive classes taught by the same teachers, but it is less well taken into account in other circumstances. This omission frequently brings forward criticisms of bad teaching at the previous stage or in the previous year, but what is more likely than bad teaching is lack of overall planning in a school or consultations between schools.

Horizontal relationships are concerned with objectives which are being pursued in two or more areas of the curriculum. These may be knowledge objectives concerned with the development of certain concepts, or they may be intellectual skills such as analysis, synthesis and evaluation, or group skills, research skills, or certain attitudes or values. Horizontal relationships are usually termed integration, which in practice often means putting two or more subjects together. Teachers interpreting integration in this way are often disappointed with the results, perhaps because they have not fully considered what aspects or elements are to be integrated or even what they mean by integration. A view of integration presented here is that the objectives can serve as integrating elements in the curriculum and that integration does not refer only to knowledge but may relate to skills, attitudes and values which are being developed in more than one area of the curriculum. For example, the ability to evaluate the relevancy of data, is an objective which could be

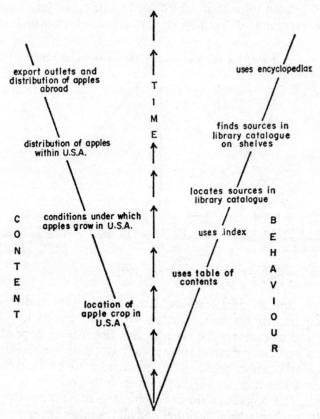

Objective: to find information about apple crop production in U.S.A. from a variety of sources

Figure 5.   Example of vertical relationships

pursued in several curriculum areas. The type of data will vary from one area to the other but the mental skills involved are likely to be very similar, and if the skills are learned and used in a number of curriculum areas pupils are likely to perform the skills more effectively (see Figure 6). The same would be so in the case of objectives such as the ability to recognise logical fallacies in reasoning, or to distinguish between facts and inferences or to predict future consequences implied in data. Affective objectives, such as to co-operate in group activities or to show reliance in working independently could be treated in a similar way.

The purpose of this chapter has been to indicate the many factors related to method which need to be taken into account in the planning of learning opportunities which will lead to

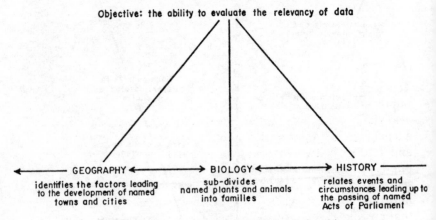

Objective: the ability to evaluate the relevancy of data

GEOGRAPHY — identifies the factors leading to the development of named towns and cities

BIOLOGY — sub-divides named plants and animals into families

HISTORY — relates events and circumstances leading up to the passing of named Acts of Parliament

Figure 6   Example of horizontal relationships

effective and efficient learning. Knowledge, skills and insights are required by teachers, together with a willingness to experiment and to evaluate the experiments. Belief in or dependence upon a particular method is inappropriate; decisions to adopt a particular method based on emotion need to be replaced by decisions based on a range of factors, fully and seriously considered. The objectives are one factor, the content another, the pupils, teacher, school, facilities and all the other elements in the total situation are others. They all have a bearing on the suitability of proposed methods.

Chapter 6

Curriculum Process: Evaluation

Teachers give considerable attention to the progress which their pupils are making. Progress is a matter with which parents are also vitally concerned; almost the first question a parent will ask a teacher is, 'How is my child getting on at school?' Both formal and informal attention is given by teachers to the matter of pupils' progress and attainment; formal attention might be regarded as the tests and examinations which are given, and informal attention as the general observation and judgements that are made. Frequently, the outcomes of both are recorded in a report which is sent home to parents.

Let us consider what the substance of this kind of assessment might be. School tests and examinations tend to be concerned with attainment in particular subjects. Close study of these tests and examinations would probably reveal that considerable attention is given to recall of facts, some attention to recall of principles, to comprehension and a little attention to application of what has been learned. The results of such examinations and tests are likely to be recorded in the form of a single mark, possibly a percentage, for each subject, with or without an indication of the pupil's position in his form for that particular subject. The implication of this kind of assessment is that each pupil is being compared with others in his form, that attention is being given only to intellectual attainment and that the marks recorded are absolute measures. Alongside the mark on the report form might be a comment, frequently remarking on the pupil's attitude to the subject, sometimes on his progress or lack of it and sometimes on his industry or lack of it. Such comments reflect the teacher's informal assessment. In addition, the form teacher usually makes an overall comment, summing up the results of the examination and adding observations on such matters as behaviour, appearance, attendance and out-of-school activities like sports, drama and service to the school.

What kind of impression does this type of assessment give? It suggests that the school is concerned very largely with the acquisition of certain knowledge and skills, mainly in the form of recall of facts and some principles, and comprehension with some application of these, and that some little and almost casual attention is given to the development of certain attitudes and to pupils' physical and social development. It is a well-known fact that those aspects of the curriculum which receive the focus of attention in examinations, whether these are internal or external, also receive the focus of attention in teaching and learning. Are schools concerned only with the aspects of education just mentioned in the kind of proportion suggested? Discussions with teachers lead one to believe that they are concerned with a whole range of objectives: the development of a variety of ways of thinking and mental skills, attitudes, values, a whole range of social, emotional and physical skills, as well as the acquisition of a body of knowledge.

Some teachers believe that some of these objectives cannot be measured and that they are very long-term so that only when the pupils become adult can we know whether schools have been successful. It is acknowledged that it is extremely difficult to measure progress towards some objectives but this is not a reason for not trying. The argument about the long-term nature of objectives might best be answered by a comparison with gardening. If a gardener plants something, no matter how slow-growing he knows it to be, he would surely become worried if he could see no signs of growth at all. So it is with many objectives: one might expect people to make further progress towards these perhaps even throughout life, but if some development cannot be seen at school there is no way of knowing whether the school is working successfully along its chosen lines.

It has already been suggested that teachers are concerned that their pupils progress towards a wide range of objectives, but the corollary to this is that assessment should be as wide in its scope as is the range of objectives. This point will be developed later.

Underlying most assessment undertaken in schools is the assumption that the curriculum is 'right'. If pupils do badly in tests and examinations it is because something is wrong with these, or at most because they are in the wrong form. Where any kind of assessment of the curriculum is carried out it tends to be of a most general kind and many teachers comment in terms of the extent to which the pupils enjoyed it or to which it 'seemed' to achieve the desired ends. Moreover, even where innovations based on a wide range of objectives have been introduced it is not uncommon for only the cognitive aspects to be assessed, often in the form of 'traditional' examinations.

Curriculum development is concerned with the planning of learning opportunities which will best give pupils the chance to make progress towards stated objectives considered desirable. Assumptions underlying this approach are that the curriculum can be improved and that pupils' progress towards the objectives is the main criterion for determining the success of the curriculum. An important difference from the kind of assessment already discussed is that the pupil is not measured against other pupils but instead he is measured against himself.[1] If a course were directed to the achievement of, say, six objectives, then pupils' progress towards all six should be 'measured' in some way.

Some writers, for example Wiseman and Pidgeon,[2] suggest that the relative importance of each objective should be decided and this should then be reflected in the assessment. For instance, in a course with six objectives emphasis could be as follows: Objective 1—25 per cent, objective 2—25 per cent, objective 3— 15 per cent, objective 4—15 per cent, objective 5—10 per cent, objective 6—10 per cent. This is an approach which has been adopted by at least one examinations board. In their Advanced Level science examinations, the Joint Matriculation Board lists abilities which are to be tested and these are grouped under six main headings as follows: knowledge, comprehension, application, evaluation and investigation, expression and experimental skills. Each of these main headings is broken down into a number of abilities. The weighting of these abilities is then indicated. In the written examination a suggested allocation is: knowledge 40 per cent, comprehension 30 per cent, application 20 per cent, evaluation and investigation 10 per cent, with a special note about expression.

[1] It is recognised that for some purposes it may be necessary to compare one pupil with others, or a group with another or against some norm.

[2] S. Wiseman and D. Pidgeon, *Curriculum Evaluation* (N.F.E.R., 1970).

However, this particular example, although including a wider range of objectives than is usual in an external examination, is not concerned with all objectives which teachers consider to be important and which we have acknowledged are not easy to assess. It must be recognised from the outset that once we venture into the area of objectives concerned with the development of interests, attitudes and values there are few, if any, techniques available for assessing progress towards these and it will be necessary for teachers to devise their own. This means, firstly, that teachers will have to learn how to do this, and, secondly, that the devices thus constructed are likely to be unsophisticated, perhaps even crude. But a start must be made and indeed has been made. Many of the Schools Council projects now have evaluation units attached to them and the work done in these may prove to be of general value.

In the meantime, let us consider the kind of techniques which teachers might devise themselves and which can be administered without too much difficulty. Firstly, it must be remembered that it is not necessary for all tests to be of the pencil-and-paper type. In many cases these are quite inappropriate. Any situation in which pupils display the behaviour indicated in the objective can be used for assessment. The situation may be one introduced specially for the purpose of assessment or it may be part of the curriculum and be used additionally for assessment.

It was stated earlier that objectives, when written with adequate clarity and precision, offer suggestions for assessment. Let us examine again the example objectives on page 41 to see what this means in practice.

Objective 1 Name in French articles of common use in the classroom
This is a fairly clear objective and perhaps provides sufficient guidance for course planning, but when it comes to assessment greater clarity becomes necessary. A decision must be made as to how many articles the pupil must name before he can be said to have achieved this objective and therefore for the curriculum to be satisfactory in this respect. The number arrived at will depend on a number of factors, including the length of time pupils have been studying French, and the amount of time in the course devoted to this objective. However, when a de-

cision has been made the objective might then read: Pupils will name in French at least twelve articles of common use in the classroom.

If the same objective were to be included over a period of time, the minimum number of items might be increased, of course. Having made this clarification, the teacher then provides opportunities for pupils to name the articles.

Objective 2 Write reports of field-study trips
As it stands this objective is indicating that any report, however short, however badly written and whatever its omissions, is acceptable as evidence of its achievement. If this is the case, the objective is adequate as it stands. If certain features are to be included in the report the objective will have to be modified. It might then read: Pupils will write reports of field-study trips. The reports will include the purpose of the study, the main findings, and the conclusion to be drawn from the findings. Criteria have now been established and reports can now be examined to determine whether they measure up to these. Additional criteria might indicate the number of such reports and the length of them.

Objective 3 Find information from a variety of sources
This objective requires greater precision. Which sources of information and how many? Does the pupil have to be able to find information from all those sources indicated? Does he have to *do* anything with the information found? Rewritten this objective might become: Pupils will find and incorporate into a report information on a given topic from encyclopedias, periodicals, textbooks and newspapers. They must use at least two of the listed sources. Assessment is then fairly straightforward. A task can be set in which pupils are asked to find information on a certain topic, listing their sources of reference. Further refinement of this objective might be made to raise the level of the behaviour required. Criteria relating to the suitability of the information or the form in which it is written might be included.

Objective 4 Read books for pleasure in their own time
and
Objective 8 Join in out-of-school activities
These both require similar clarification. How many books must

be read and how many out-of-school activities should be joined before pupils can be said to have achieved these objectives? In the case of objective 4 pupils might be asked at the beginning of a course to keep a record of books read voluntarily at home and the teacher can refer to this for evidence. Objective 8 can be assessed by consultation with colleagues; it is likely that such an objective would be a school-wide one and steps could be taken in advance to keep records of membership of out-of-school activities and so assessment would be fairly straightforward.

Objective 5 Show increasing sensitivity towards other people
This objective was discussed at some length earlier and a possible breakdown was suggested as follows—pupils will show increasing sensitivity towards other people so that they:

(*a*) Listen to the opinions of others in their group.
(*b*) Help members of their group to carry out tasks.
(*c*) Take part in community service activities.
(*d*) Criticise social practices which show lack of consideration for others.
(*e*) Propose alternative practices to those in (*d*) above.

For purposes of assessment some criterion for successful achievement of each of these five objectives must be decided. Is it sufficient that the pupil displays the behaviour once, or twice or five times during the course? Or are we concerned that each pupil should show the behaviour more frequently at the end of the course than at the beginning? In either case a modification of the objectives is necessary for assessment, e.g.:

(*a*) Listen increasingly to the opinions of others in their group.
(*b*) Increasingly help members of their group to carry out tasks.
(*c*) Take part in community service activities on at least three occasions during the year.
(*d*) Criticise increasingly social practices which show lack of consideration for individuals.
(*e*) Increasingly propose alternative practices to those in (*d*) above.

Objectives (*a*) and (*b*) can be assessed by the teacher observing the pupils and recording on a rating scale the extent of their listening and helping. Assessment of objective (*c*) could take place by keeping records of pupils' participation in community service activities. Objectives (*d*) and (*e*) could be assessed by means of rating of pupils in discussion or by means of specially set written work, or even by dramatic means through role-playing.

Objective 6 Display increasing understanding of the self
What does this objective mean? It is a long-term objective with which all stages of education are likely to be concerned and which will be pursued through many areas of the curriculum. It will, therefore, have different meanings according to the age of the pupils and according to the area of the curriculum concerned.

In a Home Economics course for adolescent pupils the objective might be interpreted in the following way—pupils will develop increased understanding of the self so that they:

(*a*) Identify their own physical type from a selection presented.
(*b*) Select an outfit of clothes best suited to their type.
(*c*) List at least four reasons for their choice in (*b*).
(*d*) Formulate two rules for choosing clothes for each physical type.

The objective is now in a suitable form to guide both course planning and assessment. All aspects of the objective might be assessed in one situation in which pupils are presented with illustrations and descriptions of the main physical types. They are then asked to identify their own type and plan an outfit best suited to their type, giving reasons for their choice and listing two rules for choice of clothes for each physical type.

Objective 7 Work together productively in groups
Assessment of this objective hinges on the meaning of 'productively'. For course planning purposes the objective is adequate, but for assessment further clarification is necessary. The objective might be broken down in a similar way to objective 5. Pupils will work together productively in groups so that they:

(*a*) Complete the task in hand.
(*b*) Offer suggestions in planning the work.
(*c*) Help others in the group.
(*d*) Listen to suggestions from others.
(*e*) Find solutions to conflicts.

An important difference between these subdivisions and those in objective 5 is that these together constitute what the teacher considers to be productive group work, while the others represent aspects of sensitivity each being assessed separately. In this case a single rating-scale might be devised and pupils placed on it according to their behaviour in all subdivisions.

Objective 9 *Practise good habits of hygiene*

Like several of the example objectives this is rather vague and the question 'Which habits of hygiene are to be practised?' must be answered. These must be identified both for purposes of course planning and assessment and then it becomes a fairly straightforward matter of observation in school, with supplementary evidence from pupils' writing, perhaps in the form of diaries or accounts of what they do before going to bed or between getting up and coming to school, or on other appropriate occasions.

Objective 10 *Swim at least twenty-five yards*

As it stands without reference to stroke, style or time this objective requires only provision of the opportunity to carry out the behaviour and assessment is simple.

Most of the above example objectives are concerned only with behaviour and not with subject-matter and could, therefore, be pursued through many areas of the curriculum. Objectives of this type were chosen as examples to illustrate a number of points; in this chapter they are used, among other purposes, to show how certain kinds of behaviour might be assessed. In the case of objectives concerned with subject-matter other points must be taken into consideration. There are two aspects of objectives of this kind—the behaviour the pupils are to show and the subject-matter itself. These may at first be listed separately, as in the following example of a unit on the blood.

Objectives   1. Know facts and principles
              2. Understand facts and principles
              3. Apply principles to new situations
              4. Interpret data

Subject-matter A. Composition of the blood
              B. Functions of the blood
              C. Circulatory system
              D. Lymphatic system

In both cases, each heading could well be broken down into further subdivisions, but for the purpose of illustrating a point here this is not necessary. For assessment purposes the objectives and subject-matter are brought together, perhaps in a table like the following.

OBJECTIVES

		1 Know facts and principles	2 Understand facts and principles	3 Apply principles	4 Interpret data
S U B J E C T M A T T E R	A Composition of blood	3	3	2	
	B Functions of blood	5	8	5	4
	C Circulatory system	4	7	5	4
	D Lymphatic system	3	2	3	2
	Total number of test items	15	20	15	10

Table 1. Test items for a unit on the blood

The number in each cell shows the number of test items allocated to each objective. For example, out of the sixty items, fifteen will test the objective: know facts and principles—three related to composition of the blood, five to functions of the blood, four to the circulatory system and three to the lymphatic system. The total in each column indicates the emphasis given to each objective and this emphasis should be reflected in the learning activities during the unit.[1]

The consideration of methods of assessing the example objectives discussed above illustrates several points. One of the most important of these is that at the point of thinking about assessment we are forced to clarify the objective. In several of the examples quoted we saw how the objective was expressed with sufficient clarity to provide guidance in course writing, but only objective 10 was sufficiently precise and clear for assessment purposes. It is not without significance that objective 10 is concerned with physical activity which is comparatively easy to describe.

The suggestions for assessment techniques indicate that a variety of devices can be appropriate: rating scales, teacher observations, diaries, written reports, pupils' records, role-playing. Other devices might include interviews, questionnaires, examination of pupils' work in art, crafts, music etc., essays.

In fact, any device which shows evidence of the behaviour indicated in the objective is an appropriate means of assessment. Many of the assessment techniques suggested can be carried out as an integral part of a course and not as special assessment 'sessions'. The important point to bear in mind is that the occasion chosen for assessment purposes must be one which evokes the behaviour which is being assessed. An example might illustrate this point.

Objective 5(*d*). Pupils will criticise increasingly social practices which show lack of consideration for individuals. The occasion chosen for assessing this objective would have to be structured most carefully. It would not be sufficient for the situation simply to provide the opportunity for pupils to criticise social practice; the situation would have to positively evoke the behaviour. A number of case histories might be presented, suitable films might be shown, dramatised cases might be presented, after which pupils are put in the 'test situation' and asked to discuss the cases or write about them according to the

---

[1] For discussion of assessment of subject-matter see N. E. Gronlund, *Stating Behavioral Objectives for Classroom Instruction* (Collier Macmillan, 1970); R. W. Tyler, *Basic Principles of Curriculum and Instruction* (University of Chicago Press, 1969); Wiseman and Pidgeon (*op. cit.*).

method of assessment (see page 75). It goes without saying that the cases chosen will be good and clear examples of social practices showing lack of consideration for individuals.

Another point to be borne in mind is that care must be taken to ensure that simple recall is not being assessed where this is not required. It is required in objective 1, for example, but in objective 5(*d*), for instance, much more than recall is required. The 'test situation', therefore, will contain new examples not previously encountered by the pupils.

Before leaving the question of assessment techniques some discussion of sampling seems relevant. In a course designed for the achievement of certain objectives pupils will be given many opportunities to display the behaviour described in the objectives. It is unrealistic to expect records to be kept of each example of behaviour and so the principle of sampling is applied. Occasions are chosen, as indicated above, in which pupils have excellent opportunities to display the appropriate behaviour and these are taken to be samples of their behaviour, the assumption being that this is representative of the pupils' behaviour on other occasions. (This is a usual procedure in examinations. Questions are based on a sample of the syllabus and the assumption is that candidates who perform well on this sample are likely to perform well on the un-sampled part of the syllabus.) For this assumption to have any validity at all, extreme care needs to be taken in the choice of occasions to be used for assessment purposes, as was suggested earlier.

There is another aspect of sampling which can be considered for use in some circumstances. If the assessment is to be used only for curriculum improvement then the principle of sampling may be applied to pupils. Detailed observations of pupils is time consuming and where this is the technique for assessment it may be considered appropriate to observe only a sample of the pupils, the assumption here being that their behaviour is representative of the behaviour of the whole class. Again, care must be taken in the choice of sample; it must be representative of the class in characteristics which are considered to be relevant to the objective being assessed. For example, in the case of objective 5(*a*), listen increasingly to the opinions of others in their group, a representative sample of pupils might include both boys and girls, pupils who are normally quiet and those who normally tend to have a lot to say, pupils who tend to be aggressive and those who tend to be placid. A sample of quiet, placid girls would not be an appropriate sample, nor would a sample of talkative, aggressive boys.

For whatever purpose or purposes assessment is being carried out it is essentially a matter of looking at pupils for evidence of progress towards objectives. This suggests that assessment needs to be undertaken on more than one occasion and a comparison made between the scores. For most purposes assessment of each objective at the beginning of a course and again at the end would be appropriate, but with regard to objectives concerned with relationships with others it might be felt that further occasions would provide a fairer assessment.

It has been suggested on several occasions in this chapter that assessment can be used for several purposes, which fall into two main categories, to provide evidence about pupils and to provide evidence about the curriculum. The same evidence may be used for both these major purposes.

Curriculum development is concerned, as we have previously indicated, with improving the curriculum and pupils' progress towards objectives is the main criterion for judging its success. So far we have discussed the importance of deciding what to measure and of finding or devising appropriate techniques for measurement, but assessment itself does not constitute evaluation. Judgement is involved in evaluation and so the further steps of interpretation and the taking of appropriate action must follow.

As an example, to illustrate these points, let us consider an experimental course which has been tried out with two groups, each of 30 pupils, in a school. The course is based on five objectives, each of which was assessed for every pupil at the beginning of the course and again at the end (1st and 2nd testing). The results of this assessment in tabulated form are shown in Table 2.

Objective 1 is assessed by means of a criterion test, where pupils are to achieve a certain standard in order to achieve this objective (Cf. objective 1 page 72). The results of this test are expressed in terms of pass (P) or fail (F).

Objectives 2–5 are assessed by means of 20-point rating scales.

The first decision to be made is what constitutes progress in the case of the objectives assessed by rating scales. This decision should be made without regard to the scores in Table 2 so that

	TESTING	OBJECTIVES 1		2		3		4		5	
		1st	2nd	1st	2nd	1st	2nd	1st	2nd	1st	2nd
PUPILS	1	F	P	4	7	9	11	7	12	9	12
	2	F	P	3	8	11	14	6	8	4	8
	3	F	P	7	9	10	12	2	9	6	9
	4	F	P	5	11	8	9	4	10	7	11
	5	F	F	2	8	7	8	9	10	4	6
	6	F	F	9	14	12	13	11	14	5	7
	7	P	P	6	8	8	10	8	12	8	12
	8	F	P	8	15	9	12	3	8	7	9
	9	F	P	1	6	15	16	6	10	8	13
	10	F	P	4	8	14	15	10	15	7	12
	58	P	P	8	14	12	14	12	16	11	13
	59	F	P	10	16	17	19	7	11	9	14
	60	F	F	2	9	9	12	8	14	8	13

Table 2. Pupils' scores in an experimental course

the decision is not influenced by the actual results. In our example, let us take an increase of three points as an indication of progress. The argument for this might be that differences of one or two points might be the result of teacher inconsistency and three points is a minimum acceptable as an indication of

		OBJECTIVES 1	2	3	4	5	TOTAL
PUPILS	1	P	1	1	1	1	5
	2	P	1	1	0	1	4
	3	P	1	0	1	1	4
	4	P	1	1	1	1	5
	5	F	1	0	0	0	1
	6	F	1	0	1	0	2
	7	P	0	0	1	1	3
	8	P	1	1	1	0	4
	9	P	1	0	0	1	3
	10	P	1	0	1	1	4
	58	P	1	0	0	0	2
	59	P	1	0	1	1	4
	60	P	1	1	1	1	5
		52	48	20	30	40	
		87%	80%	33%	50%	67%	

Table 3. Pupils' progress in an experimental course

progress. (It could be argued, of course, that even three points is inconclusive evidence, but the course is experimental in its first trial and so on this occasion arguments for three points could be supported).

On the basis of this decision a table showing progress can be constructed, with 0 indicating lack of progress and 1 indicating progress (Table 3). The column on the right indicates for each pupil the number of objectives in which progress has been made or a pass achieved and the totals at the bottom indicate the number and percentage of pupils making progress or passing in each objective.

What does this evidence indicate and what kind of action might result from it? Do the scores suggest that we can feel satisfied with the effectiveness of the experimental course? Let us consider each aspect of it in turn.

The first objective appears to be the one where most progress has been made; 87 per cent of the pupils reached the criterion set, so perhaps we can feel highly satisfied with this result. However, further consideration ought to be given to the criterion itself. Is it too low, perhaps? Further examination of Table 2 shows that very few pupils reached the criterion at the beginning of the course—only 5 out of the total of 60. At the outset 8 per cent of the pupils satisfied the criterion and at the end 87 per cent. If the criterion is judged to be at the right level, the course appears to be highly successful in relation to this objective. The fact that five pupils reached the criterion before the course started reveals one of the weaknesses of this form of assessment and indicates that *for this particular objective* the experimental course has nothing to offer these pupils. One would expect teachers to make appropriate modifications to the course so that these five pupils would either be given opportunities for reaching a higher level in the particular objective or for spending more time practising behaviour where they were experiencing difficulties, whichever was considered to be the more suitable course of action.

The results for objective 2 appear to be highly satisfactory, particularly for the first trial of a new course: 80 per cent of the pupils have made progress towards this objective.

Results for objectives 3 and 4 are less satisfactory: 33 per cent and 50 per cent respectively. Further evidence must be sought here since there must be cause for concern about these objectives. The same might also be true in the case of the fifth objective: by comparison with the first two objectives, progress here does not appear to be satisfactory.

We must turn to the teachers for further evidence. The teachers who have used the experimental course will have much to offer in the interpretation of the assessment, particularly if they have kept appropriate records, which is a wise thing to do under any circumstances but particularly when using a new course. These teachers will have carried out the assessment and may or may not have constructed the course under consideration: when asked to suggest explanations for the comparative lack of progress towards objectives 3, 4 and 5 their answers might include the following.

Not enough opportunities were given for practising the behaviour in those objectives.
The materials relating to the objectives were too difficult.
There were insufficient different ways of achieving those objectives.
The materials connected with those objectives were not sufficiently stimulating.
Some learning experiences were presented in the wrong order.
I think the pupils made more progress in this objective than the rating scale indicated.
I had difficulty placing pupils on the scale.
The situation selected for assessment was not very suitable.
I wasn't really sure what that objective meant.

Informal assessment of this kind carried out by teachers using new courses is a vital part of curriculum evaluation. It offers suggestions about the educational soundness of the course and provides valuable evidence for future action. The comments above suggest that faults might lie in three areas: in the content, materials and methods of the course; in the methods of assessment; and in the formulation of the objectives. Of these, the first is likely to be the most common, but whichever is the case action is the next step. This is the feedback aspect of curriculum development and illustrates its cyclical nature which was mentioned earlier.

Table 3 illustrates another important point, already touched upon in a different context above. Some pupils, for example pupils 5, 6 and 58, have made progress in no more than two objectives. This means that the new course was not providing opportunities for these pupils to make progress in even half of the course objectives, although it was successful with other pupils. The matter of individual differences has already been discussed at some length and the implication of the scores of pupils 5, 6 and 58 is that the curriculum was not 'right' for them and so ways should be sought by which these pupils may also make progress towards the objectives. The same argument holds for all those pupils who failed to make progress in any objective.

As well as its use in curriculum improvement assessment of this kind may also be used to provide evidence for more adequate marking and reporting on pupils. The futility of introducing new courses based on a wide range of objectives and then examining only a limited number of objectives has already been mentioned. Scores similar to those on page 81 provide a variety of evidence about pupils. If the objectives are considered to be worthwhile then evidence of pupils' progress towards them must also be worthwhile. Although the scores on page 81 have little meaning when taken on their own, being in single figures or in terms of pass or fail, taken together, they provide a profile showing strengths and weaknesses over a range of behaviours.

The question of reports for the information of parents has already been discussed briefly and reference has been made to the limitations and deficiencies of these. The form of reports is a matter for schools to decide but it is suggested that if education is to be really concerned with a wide range of objectives and is not simply paying lip-service to these, parents have a right to know how their children are progressing towards them. It would not be difficult for reports to be devised which would indicate this, providing the assessment was continually being carried out.[1] Moreover, it could be argued that parents and pupils and other interested parties such as local authorities, ratepayers and employers have a right to know how successful a school is in achieving its stated objectives, especially in the case of new and experimental curricula.

[1] See Gronlund (*op. cit.*).

Chapter 7

Contributing Disciplines

Curriculum development can be regarded as an integrative study in the sense that knowledge from the main disciplines of education is brought to bear in many aspects of curriculum planning. Moreover, curriculum planning provides the opportunity for theories to be put to the test in a practical situation.

The philosophy of education is sometimes seen as a highly academic study which has little to offer to the teacher in the practical situation. While it is true that philosophy is a highly academic study, it does have something of practical value to offer to teachers. One of its most important functions is to help teachers to think more clearly about educational matters. Many people connected with education have a tendency to use terms loosely or vaguely, and so educational philosophy by its emphasis on clarity and precision is valuable in helping to establish what is really meant. What do we mean, for instance, when we speak of integration, child-centred education, discovery learning or moral education? What do we mean when we speak of learning, teaching or discipline? Clarification of ideas about such matters is a major step towards more effective curriculum planning.

In the consideration of objectives, the philosophy of education can be very helpful, partly because of its emphasis on clarification of meanings already mentioned, and partly because educational philosophers have given much thought to the aims of education and their writings in this area will offer considerable guidance to and induce deep thinking on the part of teachers undertaking a serious study of this aspect of curriculum development.

It is likely that when teachers are considering objectives for their school or for a particular course of study, they will find they have a very long list of objectives they consider to be desirable and worthwhile for their pupils. This initial list may well be too long for possible achievement and so some kind of selection may have to be made. One factor to be borne in mind in making such a selection would be the relative importance attached to the particular objectives by the teachers concerned. This would involve making value judgements, and philosophy has a part to play in the clarification of these.

Again, when teachers are devising learning opportunities they need to ask themselves many questions, for example the question 'What shall I teach?' where the analyses and discussions of philosophers on such matters as the nature of knowledge and the whole concept of education can help to provide an answer.

Time spent on thinking out such matters will be well spent and is likely to save considerable waste of later efforts. Unfortunately not all teachers have had the kind of philosophical training to enable them to ask appropriate questions, let alone to answer them in terms likely to be helpful. To remedy this, however, there is a considerable literature available for study. A group of teachers undertaking curriculum development would find it of extreme value to have a philosopher in their group at the crucial points in their work when decisions about objectives, content and methods were being made, to help them clarify their meanings and intentions and consider the value judgements being made by asking appropriate questions at appropriate times.

Similarly, an educational psychologist could be most helpful to teachers carrying out curriculum development, but perhaps teachers are more knowledgeable in this field since educational psychology features more prominently in teacher training courses and so may require the advice of psychologists less than that of philosophers.

Psychology can offer some guidance in the selection of objectives. Knowledge of child development and of what children can learn might indicate whether the objectives proposed are realistic for the pupils for whom they are intended.

In the planning of learning opportunities knowledge derived from educational psychology will have to be taken into account. One consideration is likely to be concerned with the vital matter of motivation. Under what circumstances are pupils likely to respond best? Are these the same for all pupils? These are among the questions curriculum developers need to answer.

They are concerned also with the whole question of individual differences and how best to provide for these in learning situations. It has been suggested earlier that teachers readily acknowledge that pupils are different but find difficulty in translating this fact into practical terms in the curriculum.

Content needs to be ordered in such ways that pupils may learn it and there are various theories of learning which suggest how this might best be done. The development of skills, including intellectual ones, and attainment of attitudes and values are all objectives, and indications as to how these might be pursued can be sought from certain aspects of educational psychology.

Studies of such topics as group dynamics, interaction of teachers and pupils, personality development, problem solving, attention, the role of language in learning and methods of assessment are just some of those which are of relevance to curriculum development, along with those already mentioned. Several points need to be made about these and similar topics.

If teachers are to plan effective curricula for all their pupils it is not sufficient that they should simply recognise the existence of certain factors, they must take them into account in curriculum planning. It is of little value, for instance, to know that certain pupils are allowed to run freely at home with little supervision and cannot concentrate on anything for very long, and then to make no provision for this fact in the curriculum.

Another point to bear in mind is that there is still considerable difference of opinion in many areas of educational psychology and much that is not yet known. Care should therefore be taken in applying 'findings' indiscriminately or uncritically. Discovery learning is a case in point where considerable disagreement among psychologists still exists and yet it is widely accepted by curriculum developers and teachers as the most effective way of learning.

Moreover, some methods or techniques are adopted on the basis of a small number of experiments, not always well constructed, or on the basis of popular approbation with no 'scientific' basis at all. It is not being suggested that nothing should be tried until it has been fully supported by experiment, but only that teachers should bear in mind that sometimes they are just testing a hypothesis about something that might work under certain circumstances.

Certain aspects of educational psychology are not in dispute, however, and these can offer guide-lines and suggestions to teachers in curriculum planning. These would include, for example, the role of interest in learning, the importance of the active participation of learners, and variations in personality, rate of learning, span of concentration and interests.

Knowledge of the sociology of education is also of value to teachers in their curriculum planning. It can help teachers, for instance, to analyse the possible future aspects of society which need to be taken into account in the selection of objectives. A study of the particular social background of pupils can suggest which objectives might be given special emphasis for particular pupils.

Sociology can also help teachers to understand how the social background of pupils can influence their learning. The kinds of social experiences pupils have result in their bringing something to the learning situation which teachers need to know and take into account in curriculum planning. It also means that learning opportunities devised by the teacher are likely to have different meanings for pupils according to their previous social experiences. Knowledge of pupils' social background will suggest, in general terms, something about the pupils' interests, needs, attitudes and values and will enable teachers to anticipate to a certain extent the kind of curriculum which will be relevant for them. Naturally, general trends of this kind have to be verified and clarified by a closer study of the particular pupils before detailed curriculum plans can be made, but knowledge of this kind can help teachers to devise learning opportunities which are meaningful to the pupils.

The part to be played by a knowledge of the history of education in curriculum planning is perhaps smaller than that of the other disciplines of education. However, a knowledge of what the curriculum of the past has been and an analysis of this knowledge might enable teachers to decide what aspects, if any, can be used in the present. There is a tendency among some educationists to assume that all aspects of past curricula, sometimes termed 'traditional' are to be condemned, while present aspects, termed 'progressive' are to be advocated. On the other hand, a small number of educationists regard everything 'traditional' as desirable and to be perpetuated. Neither extreme position reflects the true situation and a close analysis of past curriculum plans should suggest what aspects might have a part to play in future planning.

The brief outline[1] in this chapter indicating the contributions to curriculum development to be made by the disciplines of education has been included to show the integrating function of curriculum development activities. Frequently, students and teachers regard their study of these disciplines largely as academic and of little practical value. In curriculum development activities, however, each discipline, to a varying extent, has an important practical function.

[1] For a more detailed and wider discussion see J. F. Kerr (ed.), *Changing the Curriculum* (University of London Press, 1968).

Chapter 8

Some Current Educational Practices

At any particular time certain educational terms and practices become popular. At the present time we hear frequently of the integrated day, vertical grouping, projects, environmental studies, de-streaming and integrated courses. The impression could be gained that these terms relate to quite definite practices but this is not the case. Not only do they mean quite different things to different people, but they are often taken to imply much more than they actually do. Moreover, it is sometimes claimed that there is a particular way of carrying them out.

For instance, the *essential* feature of the integrated day is that time is not broken up into periods for particular areas of the curriculum, but it is often taken to mean much more than this. It is sometimes thought that it must be linked with vertical grouping, or that all pupils have to work on individual assignments, or that subjects need to be integrated, or that work areas for certain subjects have to be set up, or that the role of the teacher is solely to structure the environment.

Vertical grouping means only that pupils of different ages are put together in the same class, yet it is sometimes taken to mean that pupils have to be vertically grouped within the class, or that pupils must always work co-operatively, or that there must necessarily be free movement of pupils and free availability of materials.

Projects have been in and out of educational fashion over a long period of time yet if teachers were asked what a project is or what characteristics all projects must have, a wide range of very different concepts would be revealed, the label 'project' being attached to many different practices. The label tells little or nothing of what would be seen by an onlooker viewing a project in action. However, it is not unknown for headteachers or advisers to suggest that a particular 'project' should be undertaken without reference to the situation in which it is to operate or to the curriculum pattern into which it is intended to fit.

Similarly with environmental studies, it is not always clear where these fit into the overall curriculum pattern. It would seem, at times, that care is not taken to link the vehicle of study with the specific and overarching objectives to be attained, that it is included in the curriculum because of fashion and that it is taught in a particular way because of an assumption that there is a way of teaching environmental studies that can be isolated from objectives and the situation.

Organising a school on the basis of un-streamed classes simply means that pupils are not allocated on the basis of ability. The only implication of having un-streamed classes is that this is thought or, if the hypothesis has been tested, known to help the attainment of certain objectives within a particular school situation. Other decisions concerning the functioning of the class remain to be taken.

Perhaps the greatest confusion and vagueness are associated with the term 'integrated courses'. Courses described as integrated are extremely widespread, yet rarely is there any attempt to determine what is meant by 'integrated' or to clarify what is to be 'integrated'. However, irrespective of how the word integrated is translated into educational practice it is frequently assumed that co-operative teaching as well as co-operative planning must be involved, and it is sometimes automatically linked with un-streamed groups.

In some schools some of the practices mentioned may have been adopted as a result of curriculum planning of the kind advocated in this book. In these cases, teachers are much more likely to have a clear conception of what they are doing, how they intend to do it, why they are doing it and how they will know if it is successful. Unfortunately, however, many popular practices in education tend to be adopted on less sound bases than these. Curriculum planning is often carried out on an intuitive basis, or on the basis of emotional attachments or belief or as a result of pressure. It is often felt that if many teachers are doing something or if something tends to be done in a certain way it must be 'right' or a 'good thing' and that all teachers 'ought' to be doing it. Sometimes, too, teachers develop strong emotional attachments to practices which they are unable to justify or explain rationally and which they would be reluctant to change or abandon under any circumstances.

There are occasions when teachers are subjected to strong

pressure from headteachers or advisers to adopt certain popular and fashionable practices. This appears to be the case in some schools with the introduction of un-streamed groups, where the pressure may lead to a situation in which teachers are ill-prepared as well as unwilling to teach groups with a wide range of ability.[1]

Another form of pressure, which may be less overt and more subtle, is social pressure from colleagues to adopt certain practices. Part of the satisfaction which some teachers derive from their work is of a social nature. In order to establish or maintain good social relationships with their colleagues some teachers may go along with ideas and practices suggested or used by others in the school, without questioning their educational desirability. This may be the case more particularly where some form of teacher co-operation is involved, as for instance in team teaching. A similar kind of pressure may operate in a school to encourage a newcomer to accept and follow without question an already established pattern.

Curriculum change made on the basis of intuition alone, or as a result of pressure, or because of blind faith, can all too easily have certain undesirable effects or lead to undesirable situations. A curriculum developed along one or more of these lines is hardly likely to be a coherent and consistent whole in curriculum development terms. Inconsistency could also result if individual practices are seen in isolation from the particular learning situation, from other practices, from purposes and from planned continuous progress. Additionally, an over-strong emphasis may well be placed on one aspect of the curriculum even to the exclusion of others. In the case of un-streamed groups, for instance, great attention is often given to the initial organisational factor but little attention is given to the modification of objectives, the ability of teachers to cope with the new situation, the adequacy and suitability of available resources, the possible need for new approaches to learning and teaching, or procedures for determining success.

Lack of consistency in the curriculum may take several forms. The curriculum may be inconsistent in that the objectives, content, method and assessment procedures are not inter-dependent and interrelated. Hoped-for objectives might include

[1] For an alternative approach to the introduction of un-streamed groups see H. and A. Nicholls (*op. cit.*), pp. 109–12.

social and emotional ones, while the learning opportunities make insufficient or no provision for their attainment and the assessment procedures are concerned exclusively with cognitive objectives. There might also be an inconsistency in the curriculum of a pupil or group of pupils, in that part of it is directed to the achievement of certain purposes and part of it towards opposing or conflicting purposes. It is suggested elsewhere in this book (p. 98), for example, how this may happen when courses or materials prepared outside the school are used. Even learning opportunities devised inside the school could be directed towards conflicting objectives, as could some of the particular practices of the kind already mentioned, with different teachers working towards very different ends, especially when particular practices are seen in isolation.

Another possible result of curriculum planning which has no rational, theoretical basis and in which faith and belief are predominant is the tendency to be convinced that pupils will automatically reap *unspecified* benefits from the currently popular practices used. It is often thought, for instance, that 'integrated' courses are invariably more beneficial than subject-based courses, or that all pupils will invariably benefit by being in un-streamed rather than streamed groups. On the other hand, it is sometimes thought that by using certain practices certain *specified* ends will automatically and inevitably be achieved. It is claimed, for example, that 'integrated' courses invariably lead to a unified understanding of knowledge, that environmental studies lead pupils to an awareness of and a concern for their surroundings, or that vertical grouping leads to improved social relationships. The claims are made, the beliefs are held, but evidence is not sought from assessment to support them.

The adoption of popular practices without reference to a rational basis for curriculum planning may so easily lead to naïve questions such as the following:

How do you teach five-year-old pupils?
How do you do the integrated day?
Do you think my pupils ought to do a project?
Is there a book that will tell me how to teach
environmental studies?

Questions of this kind suggest a number of underlying assumptions:

that means can be dissociated from ends;
that means can be dissociated from the situation;
that there are best ways of teaching which can be learned
in isolation and then applied in any situation;
that it is better for a teacher to be told how to teach
rather than for guide-lines to be suggested on which he
can create custom-built curricula;
that there is a way of teaching, say, five-year-olds, with
the implication that there are common aims, stereotyped
pupils and a set approach which will guarantee success
in any school.

Comment has been made so far on the basis of which popular educational practices may be introduced into the curriculum, on the fact that specific labels have been given to particular current practices which cover widely varying activities, and on some of the possible effects of these factors. We would argue that the job of a teacher has become too complicated and is too responsible for wholly intuitive approaches to curriculum development or a mere following of the latest fashion. We would hope to see a move towards a more sophisticated and more rational approach which is based on theoretical as well as practical considerations and which will lead to a greater precision in both thought and action. In carrying out curriculum planning there is a whole range of interrelated decisions to be made. A basic framework for these decisions is outlined in the early chapters of this book.[1] It may be considered desirable or helpful *after* carrying out curriculum development to give a name to the resulting learning opportunities. This is perfectly acceptable but it should be borne in mind that the name refers to learning opportunities devised for particular pupils for particular purposes in a particular situation. No doubt some of the terms mentioned earlier in this chapter and their related concepts will remain but they will be used more precisely and will be seen as part of curriculum planning as a whole without emotional attachments.

When curriculum development is viewed as having a rational and theoretical framework, the kind of questions mentioned above are likely to be replaced by questions of this kind:

For what purposes and under what situational
conditions might vertical grouping tend to be
more appropriate than age grouping?

[1] For a more extensive discussion of decision making in curriculum planning see H. and A. Nicholls (*op. cit.*) Chapter 5.

What information might be helpful to me in
deciding how to teach a group through a study
of the environment?
How can we determine whether our attempts to
teach un-streamed classes have been successful?
Bearing in mind what we hope to achieve, would
it be helpful to abandon the time-table?

It is recognised that for many teachers a popular educational
practice can provide a useful and interesting *starting-point* for
curriculum development. In discussing such a practice teachers
may come to a clearer definition of what it is and a deeper understanding of what it implies, at least as far as they are concerned.
They can discuss what purposes a particular practice is likely to
achieve, whether it is appropriate for their pupils, whether they
have adequate resources for it, what other decisions have to be
taken if it is introduced and how they will judge whether it is
successful. These are some of the major points which need to be
discussed in undertaking curriculum development.

Not all teachers have had the benefit of formal education in
curriculum development, but most recently qualified teachers
have, as part of their professional course, while many more
experienced teachers have taken in-service courses in this field.
These teachers, both newly qualified and more experienced, can
offer as their particular contribution their knowledge of the
theoretical aspects of curriculum development. Other teachers
have valuable contributions to make based on their expertise in
the classroom, their knowledge of the pupils, their ability to
devise resources or their specialism in an area of the curriculum.
Curriculum development is essentially a bringing together of
theory and practice—both must be involved. Educational
practices of the kind discussed in this chapter may remain, and
others may become popular, but they all need to be considered
against a background of curriculum theory.

Chapter 9

Some Practical Considerations

An approach to curriculum development has been presented which shows the relationship among the various elements of the curriculum: objectives, content, methods and evaluation. These elements are built into a continuous cycle of activities which constitute a process of curriculum development:

(1) Analysis of the situation.
(2) Selection of objectives.
(3) Selection and organisation of content.
(4) Selection and organisation of methods.
(5) Assessment and evaluation.

The activities in the process of curriculum development were presented in a particular order which is perhaps the most logical one and which is to be recommended, given suitable circumstances. However, certain points need to be made about this sequence.

In practice one does not move directly from one activity to the next and to the next until one reaches evaluation. Instead, there is a constant moving backwards and forwards. For instance, in considering content, there is constant reference back to objectives and forwards to methods. In considering methods constant reference is made to content and objectives. Evaluation cannot be considered without reference to objectives and content. The necessity to move backwards and forwards through the cycle indicates the very close relationships among the elements in the curriculum.

Another important consideration related to the sequence is that of a starting-point. It has been suggested that the sequence outlined in this book is probably the most logical one and should be followed where this is both possible and practicable. This might happen, for instance, where teachers are planning a completely new course, or where a new school is being opened.

Sometimes, however, teachers have a particular interest or orientation, say towards evaluation or content, and there is no reason why these should not provide a *starting-point*. The important factor to bear in mind is that it is only a starting-point and that all the other stages in the process *must* be dealt with in due course.

Teachers are frequently working in an existing situation and trying to bring about change at the same time. They cannot start with a clean slate and this may force them to begin their considerations at a point other than that which might otherwise be regarded as the logical starting-point. An examination of present content, materials and methods would lead to a clarification of objectives if teachers were to ask themselves such questions as 'Why am I teaching this?' 'What does this method imply?' Such questions might result in possible changes in content, materials and/or methods.

Brief reference was made in the opening chapter of this book to the various settings in which curriculum development might be carried out. Some further points relating to these might profitably be discussed.

The publication of Schools Council sponsored courses and materials is an important matter for teachers. Courses such as the Nuffield language courses have a statement of objectives and a series of learning situations with supporting materials and equipment; the learning opportunities are likely to be presented in a particular sequence and it is hoped that as a result of undergoing these the pupils will make progress towards the stated objectives. Whether this is what will in fact happen is dependent on a number of factors. Much will depend upon the teacher's skill in handling the new courses, which in turn is dependent upon an understanding of the relationships between objectives and learning activities. Much will also depend on the suitability of the courses for the pupils using them.

Both these factors can be controlled by a teacher who understands the relationships that exist among the elements of the curriculum and the process of curriculum development. Such a teacher would be in a position to carry out two important exercises: first, to carry out a thorough study of any new course to establish the relationships between the objectives and the learning opportunities outlined in the course, and to plan his particular approach to using the course with his own pupils within the general framework provided. Next, after using the course he would then be in a position to assess his pupils' progress towards the stated objectives and make any changes in the course he then considered appropriate. Because of his understanding of the relationships within the course any modifications he made would not affect the basis on which the course was constructed.

The matter of studying the objectives of the course to establish their compatibility with his own objectives was mentioned in the opening chapter. If there was partial compatibility but it was felt that some alterations to the objectives were desirable, a teacher with an understanding of curriculum development would realise that in changing certain objectives he would also have to change the related learning opportunities.

The Schools Council is also publishing materials rather than courses and here the problems are somewhat different. In the case of materials there are likely to be either no objectives or perhaps a small range of objectives implicit in the materials. There will be no sequence of learning opportunities and the teacher will have to build the materials into a course. The materials will have to be studied carefully on several counts. A teacher must be aware of any implicit objectives and consider whether these are appropriate and compatible with those of the school. For example, in deciding to use the Humanities materials devised by Lawrence Stenhouse, a teacher should consider whether the fact that pupils using these are encouraged to question and criticise and discuss freely is likely to cause difficulty in his school. This is not to suggest that the Stenhouse materials develop undesirable skills or attitudes, but rather that in some schools these may be in conflict with other objectives and therefore cause problems for the pupils when they go from one class to another. The responsibility is with the teacher concerned to take whatever action he considers appropriate, perhaps to work for widespread acceptance of these objectives.

Teachers using resource materials of this kind must make other decisions. If there are no stated objectives they must decide whether this is satisfactory to them or not; preferably they must study the materials and decide how learning opportunities might be devised using these materials which will lead to objectives they consider important and desirable. Alternatively, they might decide that the materials can form a useful addition to an existing course. In either case, the criteria discussed in chapter four relating to selection of content might usefully be applied to materials of this type.

Curriculum development undertaken as a group activity either in a school or a teachers' centre has many advantages. In addition to the sharing of ideas, group activity provides for an extension and development of these ideas. As an idea is offered by one member of a group it is built on and developed by others in the group. Group activity usually means that a wide variety of skills, abilities and interests needed in curriculum development are available. Some teachers might be good at preparing objectives, others at devising assessment techniques, others conversant with many audio-visual techniques, others particularly knowledgeable about child development. Some group members might display leadership skills of many kinds. Although a group might have a formal leader, individuals within the group might at various times take the leadership for different reasons: sometimes because they have special knowledge which is needed at that time or because they display a particular skill or talent when that is needed. It might be skill as a peacemaker, or ability to persuade the group to make a decision or to defer a decision until further evidence is available, or to make another member of the group feel accepted when his ideas have been rejected.

If the formal leader has sufficient knowledge and understanding of the theory and practice of curriculum development and of group dynamics, curriculum development undertaken on a group basis can serve as an admirable vehicle for in-service education. One of the problems associated with traditional in-service education of the short-course and lecture type is that its effect on classroom practice is not fully known, but may be less than the effects of co-operative curriculum development. In order to implement curriculum change teachers have to change themselves in two ways. First they need new knowledge, skills and abilities, and in addition, and these might be of greater importance, they need changed attitudes. The first of these can be acquired to some extent through traditional in-service courses, but the second may be more difficult in this way largely because it takes time to change attitudes. If a group of teachers come together to undertake curriculum development, partly because of group interaction and the influence of group members on each other, and partly because the group is likely to remain together for some time by the nature of their task, attitudes are likely to change. Any innovations proposed by the group and incorporated into the new curriculum are more likely to be accepted and subsequently implemented by group members. For example, if a group were considering the use of team teaching in a course and this was not acceptable to some members, the matter would be fully discussed with points for and against given due consideration. If the group finally agreed to incorporate team teaching the dissenting members would be likely, at the very least, to give the new course a try, because of the reasons put forward by their colleagues. In some cases dissenting members might become fully committed eventually to the idea of team teaching in the course.

The question of time is an important one in relation to curriculum development. It is not an exercise which can be undertaken in undue haste. Each stage in the cycle must be allowed sufficient time, not only in order that each step can be carried out efficiently but also so that the teachers involved can develop sufficient understanding of what they are doing, which in turn is likely to lead to positive attitudes.

This raises problems both for work in schools and in teachers' centres. If curriculum development is to be accepted as part of teachers' professional responsibility, a way must be found to make this possible. The task of curriculum development is too demanding to be undertaken at the end of a school day. Many schools and local authorities make arrangements for teachers to be released from school for a half or full day to go to work in teachers' centres, but where a whole or even part of a staff wish to undertake curriculum development the problem is greater.

This leads us to a consideration of other factors which might operate in a school and act as inhibitors of curriculum development. These are:

1. Non-availability of time
2. Headteacher imposing his views
3. Teachers who do not question
4. Teachers who know all the answers
5. Teachers who are unwilling to see another viewpoint
6. A narrow view of education
7. Strongly opposing opinions leading to stalemate
8. Unwillingness to co-operate with others

A headteacher who is inclined to impose his views on his staff and who sees himself as the sole source of educational ideas and innovation will tend to act as a very strong deterrent to the development of a balanced curriculum in his school. Fortunately, this kind of headteacher is fast disappearing from the educational scene and in many schools all members of staff are encouraged to make their contribution of ideas.

There are, however, some teachers who rarely question what they are doing. These are teachers who are teaching the same thing in the same way that they have been teaching for years. The fact that they have changed, that society is changing, that their pupils are different appears to have escaped them. Teachers should be prepared to ask themselves searching questions about the curriculum they are offering their pupils. Frequently, pupils are blamed for lack of interest or progress; some teachers never consider blaming the curriculum.

Some teachers do question, perhaps not very searchingly, and then decide that they have found 'the right answer'. Such teachers put all their faith in a particular approach which may become an end in itself rather than a means to an end. Teachers of this kind are unlikely to see another's viewpoint; they become inflexible, rigid in approach and narrow in outlook.

Other teachers might see education in a very restricted way. They might have a narrow range of objectives, stating, for example, that their main and exclusive concern is that their pupils should pass external examinations. Such teachers are unlikely to show any interest in curriculum development.

It may happen in a school that there are teachers with strongly opposing views: these might be about the purposes of education, particular approaches, content, matters of discipline or any other matters. This could lead to a situation in which nothing was done because no way could be found of modifying the views held.

If teachers are unwilling to co-operate, to share ideas and to plan and work together it will be difficult to develop a curriculum which is cohesive and consistent.

Factors such as those just outlined might be present in varying degrees in many schools. Those who can recognise them, particularly if they are in positions of influence or authority, will have to work hard to modify them if they wish to undertake curriculum development. Frontal attacks are unlikely to prove successful and so opportunities for more subtle and indirect approaches should be sought.

The ideal situation is one in which the head and staff are willing to work together to decide what they are trying to achieve and where each teacher's work both inside and outside the classroom is directly related to this. Such a situation requires much goodwill, energy and effort and needs to be supported by an organisation which makes the appropriate arrangements for the plans to be implemented.

Chapter 10

Conclusion

Children would learn even if they did not go to school. Learning in school, however, differs from learning outside in that it is structured. If pupils' learning is to be directed towards desired ends it must be planned. This book has suggested a particular approach to planning; it has not suggested what the plans should be. It is acknowledged that there are other approaches to curriculum development. However, it is argued here that curriculum planning should be undertaken on the basis of a logical and rational process. Such an approach enables teachers to cope with rapidly changing situations. It provides a framework within which rational decisions can be made and enables teachers to devise a curriculum which is as appropriate as may be for their particular pupils.

Frequently a balance has to be maintained between what is desirable and what is possible. It is rare to find a perfect situation in which ideas can be worked out to perfection. A compromise has to be made since teachers are not really free, but restricted by many aspects of the total environment. So in the end the curriculum reflects realism as well as idealism.

Curriculum development is not the prerogative or the responsibility of a few, such as the headteacher or heads of department, nor is it confined to certain kinds of schools or to certain pupils within schools. Primary school teachers using what might be called progressive or modern methods need to undertake curriculum development, since there is a need to consider objectives and since, even in what appears to be a free approach by pupils, there is a structure and there is planning. Secondary school teachers preparing pupils for external examinations can also engage in curriculum development. One way, of course, is to adopt the Mode Three form of C.S.E. examining, but another way would be to use the examining body's syllabus to achieve a wider range of objectives than knowledge to pass the examination. It should not be thought that curriculum development can only be undertaken on behalf of the non-examination pupils in a secondary school.

Participation in curriculum development activities is likely to result in teachers thinking more clearly about curriculum matters. They are more likely, for instance, to see the dangers in adopting ideas and practices which work elsewhere without subjecting them to strict scrutiny and without consideration of their suitability to their own particular situation. They are less likely to regard the decision to use vertical grouping, or to integrate the school day, or to de-stream as ends in themselves. Instead they are more likely to see these decisions as being related to other decisions and to the objectives they wish their pupils to achieve.

School-wide curriculum planning is important if the learning opportunities which are provided for pupils are to support and reinforce each other and if direct conflict and opposition of objectives is to be avoided. Communication is a vital element in curriculum planning, whether in schools or teachers' centres. It is unlikely that everyone who is ultimately to be concerned with new curricula will be present at every curriculum meeting, except perhaps in very small schools. Those teachers concerned in the planning have a responsibility not only to keep their colleagues informed about what is happening, but also to make provision for the communication to be two-way, so that colleagues' views can be heard and taken into account. Communication of this two-way nature will make acceptance of the new curricula more likely.

Curriculum development is a dynamic process. Its cyclical nature suggests that it is an activity which has no beginning and no end. The changing nature of society, schools and pupils supports the view of curriculum development as a never-ending activity. It is not an activity which can be undertaken once and then it is finished. This is not to say, necessarily, that every teacher must be engaged in curriculum development all the time, but it does mean that some aspect of curriculum development work is likely to be going on in a school most of the time. A school which is standing still in terms of its curriculum is in fact going backwards. This is not to suggest that change should be undertaken for its own sake, nor that all the change will be of a major dimension. In some years change in a particular school or class might be quite small, but change there should surely be since the pupils, the focal point of any curriculum, are not the same as in the previous year.

To undertake curriculum development in the way suggested is not an easy task, but then nothing concerned with teaching is easy. The study and practice of curriculum development is, however, most stimulating, satisfying and rewarding, second only to the actual implementation of the curriculum. It provides real purpose to the study of the major disciplines of education and offers the opportunity of putting theory to the test in a real and practical situation. No teacher who regards himself as a professional person can afford not to participate.

Primary example to illustrate curriculum process

N.B. These examples have been devised solely for the purpose of illustrating some of the major points outlined in previous chapters and the situations described are imaginary ones. If the principles of curriculum development described in this book have been fully understood and accepted it will be realised that the following examples are not intended for use by teachers unless they are modified and adapted to suit another situation. Moreover, units of this kind involve the use of certain materials and many of those included in the secondary example do not exist in reality, e.g. certain films and booklets.

SITUATION
Teacher
    Age: Forty.
    Sex: Female.
    Experience: Teaching children whose ages have ranged from 5 to 11.
    Special ability: Reasonably good at organisation.
    Disability: Very poor artistically.
    General comment: Teacher confident and sure of her discipline.

School
    Character of buildings: Old. Many odd corners which could be used for individual work, a library or small group work.

Class
    Size: Small with only twenty-five pupils.
    Content: Mixed but mainly boys.
    Ages: From six to eleven.
    I.Q.: From seventy to ninety, but most of the children between seventy and eighty.
    Reasons for being in the class: General backwardness and/or social and emotional difficulties.
    Social groupings in the class: Many isolates. Small exclusive gangs of boys and girls sometimes grouped according to family friendships existing outside the school.
    Speech: Limited and restricted in code.
    Physical make-up: Poor co-ordination and control.

Personality: Lacking in confidence. Many show marked aggressive and submissive tendencies.

Other Factors

Other teachers: Generally very helpful. A history of co-operation. One teacher particularly good in the art and craft area.

Parents: Shy. Antagonistic. Low level of literacy. Many out of work. Poor attitude to school. Large families. The successful families move out of the area. All have televisions but few bother with books. Many fathers unskilled.

Environment: A decaying part of an old town.

School apparatus: TV. Record Player. Duplicator.

Some objectives for children with special difficulties in the areas of social responsibility, acceptability and relationships:

1. accept orders from younger and/or less able children
2. offer to help others
3. listen to other pupils' ideas
4. accept as fellow workers those who are not particular friends
5. join with others to complete tasks
6. speak clearly, pleasantly and with confidence
7. help others who are less able
8. accept others who express opinions which differ from their own
9. work unsupervised, for increasingly long periods

School aims into which these objectives will fit:

   (a) to encourage an increasing ability to work with others
   (b) to encourage the social integration of isolates
   (c) to develop such skills as will make the child more readily acceptable to society as a whole

LEARNING OPPORTUNITIES

   (i) Individual mathematics assignments with the suggestion that anyone can give help or ask for help from others.

   For objectives 2, 3, 4, 7, 9.

   (ii) Group history projects with pupils of mixed skills and abilities in each group. Pupils to have limited access to teacher expert in arts and crafts.

   For all objectives.

   (iii) A scheme for helping infants with their work. In this scheme each child in the class to adopt a child in the reception class for a short period each week. The infant to be the boss and say how he wishes to be helped.

   For objectives 1, 3, 5, 7, 8, 9.

(iv) The organisation and running through committees of:
   (a) A class sports day to which parents, grown-up friends and relations are invited to watch and take part.
   (b) A visitors' afternoon when the parents, brothers, sisters, friends and relations are invited to the class to take part in class activities and have afternoon tea.

   For objectives 1, 4, 5, 6, 7, 8, 9.

(v) The running of assembly once a week with all pupils taking an active part in the organisation and presentation.

   For all objectives.

(vi) Panels of advisers to be set up for such things as writing, reading, mathematics, sewing, painting, knitting, making models. . . . These panels to be available when needed to help fellow pupils. All pupils to belong to one, but not more than two, panels.

   For objectives 4, 5, 6, 7, 8, 9.

(vii) Each child to have special social responsibilities within the school or class. These responsibilities to be such things as:
   Keeping a list of those children who come to school late.
   Collecting silver paper for the Guide Dogs Association.
   Looking after the stock cupboard.
   Giving out paint.
   Looking after visitors.
   Helping at the dinner table.
   Keeping the class tidy.
   Checking and giving out apparatus.
   Collecting information for the head as required.
   The responsibilities to be rotated.

   For objectives 1, 2, 3, 4, 5, 6, 7, 9.

(viii) Each pupil to make a 'Finding Out Book' on a topic of his own choice with one or more collaborators.

   For objectives 2, 3, 5, 9.

Note. Objective attainment is not automatic but rather depends on the teacher's ability to exploit the opportunities. It should also be remembered that the above objectives and learning opportunities relate to only part of the whole curriculum which would perhaps have more social objectives and also intellectual, emotional and physical objectives.

ASSESSMENT

Objective	*Method of Assessment*
1. accept orders from younger and/or less able children	Recorded observations by the reception class teacher helping with the

	scheme in which children go to help an infant
2. offer to help others	The headteacher to spend one day a month working with the class and making notes in this particular area
3. listen to other pupils' ideas	Teacher-recorded observation made during discussions and group work
4. accept as fellow workers those who are not particular friends	Pupils to keep a list of those with whom they have worked. These lists to be analysed by the teacher later
5. join with others to complete tasks	Pupils to keep a record of completed co-operative tasks
6. speak clearly, pleasantly and with confidence	Use tape recorder at the beginning and end of the learning period Let pupils themselves comment on the extent to which they can hear and understand what a fellow pupil says when he is performing before an audience
7. help others who are less able	Systematic teacher-recorded observation. Rating scale
8. accept others who express opinions which differ from their own	Rating scale
9. work unsupervised for increasingly long periods	Monthly teacher notes on the approximate length of time each pupil can be left to work alone away from direct supervision

Assessment notes

In the social area objective testing is difficult. A sociometric test can often be used where social interaction is to be investigated but in this particular instance it is hoped that the problem of objectivity has been overcome to some extent by using a teacher from another class to do some of the assessment, calling in the help of the headteacher, using rating scales and using a tape recorder.

The use of the headteacher and the pupils themselves will help reduce the assessment load.

From a comparison of initial and final assessments the amount of progress towards objective achievement may be obtained.

Secondary example to illustrate curriculum process

THE SITUATION

This unit was devised for a group of third year pupils in a new, well-equipped and un-streamed comprehensive school in a new town. In the school there are pupils from the original small town from which the new one has been developed, pupils from several parts of the country and a small number of coloured immigrants. The children come from a wide range of backgrounds including slum clearance areas, areas of high unemployment and professional middle-class areas.

Although the town was planned in such a way as to foster social integration and although this is one of the school's aims, the teacher of social studies became aware from pupils' writings, general conversation, contributions to discussions and from their conduct that there were very few signs that such integration was even beginning to develop. Moreover, some pupils showed signs of resentment at having had to come to live in Newtown and many seemed completely unaware of why and how the town had developed and of the ideas that had been behind the planning.

The teacher felt that knowledge of the town's development and an understanding of the planning principles underlying the development were prerequisites to the development of any positive attitudes towards the town and fellow inhabitants. It was hoped that because pupils had either come to the town fairly recently and were not fully settled or had experienced the rather sudden change from living in a small town to a large developing one the subject-matter of the unit would engage their interests. It was felt that the range of previous experiences and backgrounds, the range of attitudes towards the town and the varied reasons for living there would provide valuable learning material.

AIMS AND OBJECTIVES

Among the school aims are the following:

1. To develop feelings of loyalty to colleagues, school and town.
2. To encourage social integration.
3. To develop high personal standards of work and conduct.
4. To foster active, inquiring attitudes to study.

Bearing in mind these aims, the characteristics and backgrounds of the pupils and the resources available in the school and the town, a social studies unit was developed based on the following objectives:

1. *Knowledge of the recent historical development of Newtown so that pupils can:*
   (a) State the principal stages in the development of Newtown between 1950 and 1972.
   (b) Reproduce the reasons for the development of Newtown.
   (c) Describe the new features of the town in housing, education, recreational provision and shopping facilities.
2. *Understanding of the principles of planning applied in the development of Newtown so that pupils can:*
   (a) Outline the reasons for the location of housing estates.
   (b) Explain the reasons for the various types of housing on each estate.
   (c) Outline the reasons for the location of schools.
   (d) Explain the provision of recreational facilities.
   (e) Predict possible future provision of recreational facilities.
   (f) Explain the location of shops and shopping centres.
3. *Co-operation in group activities so that pupils will:*
   (a) Listen to the ideas and suggestions of other members of the group.
   (b) Offer suggestions and ideas to the group.
   (c) Remain calm during group discussions.
   (d) Complete tasks set by the group.
4. *Commitment to social improvement so that pupils will:*
   (a) Report an example of social deficiency or weakness.
   (b) Propose a course of action to remedy the deficiency or weakness.
   (c) Take the first step in the implementation of the action.

Materials/ equipment	Teacher activities	Pupils' activities	Objectives
I Film: The Growth of Newtown (a publicity film)	Show film	Watch film	1, 2
	Lead discussion on main points in film concerning development of Newtown	Participate in discussion	1, 2
II Pamphlets, brochures, pictures and general information from Planning Department	Arrange class in groups. (Bearing in mind the fact that the class has a range of abilities and that a major school aim is concerned with social integration the teacher arranged the groups so that	Study materials provided. Discuss planning and development of Newtown	1, 2, 3

Materials/ equipment	Teacher activities	Pupils' activities	Objectives
	they contained some intellectually bright, average and below average pupils and that the pupils came from different back-grounds)		
	Lead class to discuss some possible questions for Planning Officer in his visit to the class	Suggest questions for Planning Officer	1, 2
III	Introduce speaker, the local Planning Officer, who gives talk about planning of Newtown	Listen to speaker	1, 2
		Ask questions and join discussions with Planning Officer	1, 2, (3(a), 3(b)
IV	Plans with class next stage of work which is to study various aspects of planning e.g. shops, schools, homes, recreation facilities, in groups	Participation in planning	3(a), (b), (c)
Documents, maps, plans, brochures, booklets from Planning Department Tape Recorder, Camera Notebooks	Guides, helps, suggests, listens to plans, questions etc. as appropriate	Plan activities to study chosen aspect. These might include: visits to various parts of town, visits to Town Hall to question planning specialists, making tape recordings, taking films, preparing charts, graphs, writing reports	1, 2, 3

Materials/ equipment	Teacher activities	Pupils' activities	Objectives
V Materials prepared during previous activities	As above	Set up display of work. Talks by pupils to whole class on findings Questions and general discussion	1, 2, 3
VI	Plans with class next stage of work which is to interview other pupils and members of public about certain aspects of planning	Participate in planning	3(a), (b), (c)
	Guides, helps, suggests, listens to plans, questions etc. as appropriate	In groups plan method of interviewing and discuss questions to be asked	1, 2, 3
Tape Recorder	As above	Rehearse interviews. Carry out interviews (a) within school (b) outside school	3 3, 4(a)
VII Content of interviews	As above	Analyse interviews Discuss findings Summarise these in an appropriate form. Report back to class. Propose suitable action for deficiencies in provisions in town	3, 4(a)
VIII Content of interviews	As above	Find suitable ways of urging action on deficiencies found. These might include: writing to local councillors, letter to news-papers, petitions, interview on local	3, 4(c)

Materials/ equipment	Teacher activities	Pupils' activities	Objectives
		radio, voluntary service etc. depending on what is found and what is possible	

ASSESSMENT

Objectives 1 and 2 by means of objective tests and an examination of pupils' work.

Objective 3 by means of a 5-point rating scale. It will be noted that when pupils are working in groups the teacher is free to move around the class and is therefore in a good position to make observations.

Objective 4. Pupils to make a report of their findings and of the steps taken to initiate action either verbally or in writing, as appropriate. An objective test of social commitment will also be given.

NOTES

1. The unit provides a very general framework within which the teacher can act and make additions or modifications at the point of implementation.
2. It provides opportunities for pupils to undertake a variety of activities and for pupils to do different types of work.
3. The unit caters for individual differences in ability and interests, in that there is choice of group activities and within these for pupils to undertake particular tasks. Where content is important, as in the early stages of the unit, it is presented in a variety of ways, e.g. in a film, in pamphlets, brochures and pictures, through discussions led by the teacher and through a visiting speaker and subsequent questioning and discussion.
4. Perhaps the most important point is that the pupils do not automatically make progress towards the related objectives. A great deal depends on what the teacher does to help the pupils.
5. Another point related to the objectives is that the teacher's original concern was with pupils' lack of positive attitudes towards Newtown and their fellow inhabitants. The teacher felt that knowledge of the town's development might be a first step towards a more desirable attitude and that while social integration and feelings of loyalty were long-term aims, objectives 3 and 4 were realistic and short-term manifestations of these more complex attitudes.
6. The objective tests and rating scale are given either before the unit is started or at the very beginning, and again at the end so that each pupil's progress towards each objective can be assessed.

Short Selected Bibliography

The literature in the field of curriculum development is large and ever-increasing. For those who wish to continue their studies it is suggested that the following books might provide a useful starting-point.

Beauchamp, G. A.   *Curriculum Theory,* Kagg Press, 1968.

Doll, R. C.   *Curriculum Improvement: Decision Making and Process,* Allyn and Bacon, 1970.

Elam, S. (ed.)   *Education and the Structure of Knowledge,* Rand McNally, 1966.

Ford G. W. and Pugno, L. (eds.)   *The Structure of Knowledge and the Curriculum,* Rand McNally, 1964.

Hirst, P. H.   *Knowledge and the Curriculum,* Routledge and Kegan Paul, 1974.

Hooper, R. (ed.)   *The Curriculum: Context, Design and Development,* Oliver and Boyd, 1971.

Musgrove, S.   *Patterns of Power and Authority in English Education,* Methuen, 1971.

Phenix, P. H.   *Realms of Meaning,* McGraw Hill, 1964·

Saylor, J. G. and Alexander, W. M.   *Curriculum Planning for Modern Schools,* Holt, Rinehart, Winston, 1966

Smith, B. O., Stanley, E. and Shores, J. H.   *Fundamentals of Curriculum Development* Harcourt, Brace and World, 1957.

Taba, H.   *Curriculum Development: Theory and Practice,* Harcourt, Brace and World, 1971.

Taylor, P. H. *et al.*   *Purpose, Power and Constraint in the Primary School Curriculum,* Macmillan, 1974.

Thornton, J. W. and Wright, J. R. (eds.)   *Secondary School Curriculum,* Chas. E. Merrill, 1963. ´

Verduin, J. R.   *Co-operative Curriculum Improvement,* Prentice-Hall, 1967.

Wheeler, D. K.   *Curriculum Process,* University of London Press, 1967.

Bibliography

Bloom, B. S. *et al.*   *Taxonomy of Educational Objectives, Handbook I: Cognitive Domain*, Longmans, Green & Co., 1956.

Bruner, J. S.   *The Process of Education*, Harvard University Press, 1960.

Gronlund, N. E.   *Stating Behavioral Objectives for Classroom Instruction*, Collier Macmillan, 1970.

Kerr, J. F. (ed.)   *Changing the Curriculum*, University of London Press, 1968.

Krathwohl, D. R. *et al.*   *Taxonomy of Educational Objectives, Handbook II: Affective Domain*, Longmans, Green & Co., 1964.

Nicholls, H. and A.   *Creative Teaching*, George Allen and Unwin, 1975.

Nisbet, S.   *Purpose in the Curriculum*, University of London Press, 1968.

Schools Council   Working Paper No. 10, *Curriculum Development: Teachers' Groups and Centres*, H.M.S.O., 1967.

Tyler, R. W.   *Basic Principles of Curriculum and Instruction*, University of Chicago Press, 1969.

Wiseman, S. and Pidgeon, D.   *Curriculum Evaluation*, N.F.E.R., 1970.

Index

Creative Teaching
An Approach to the Achievement
of Educational Objectives
Audrey and Howard Nicholls

In *Creative Teaching*, Audrey and Howard Nicholls examine certain aspects of the approach to curriculum planning and develop the ideas outlined in their previous, highly successful book, *Developing a Curriculum*.

It is designed for both practising and prospective teachers who wish to keep abreast of curriculum development today.

INTRODUCCIÓN

La gramática es una herramienta fundamental en el proceso de aprendizaje y perfeccionamiento de una lengua extranjera.

Este libro va dirigido a todos aquellos estudiantes de español/LE que quieran aprender o consolidar los problemas básicos de la gramática española.

En *Breve gramática* el aprendiz de nivel básico/intermedio encontrará fácilmente la solución —de manera breve, clara y concreta— a cada uno de los problemas que pueda tener tanto en el estudio como en el uso de la lengua.

Este libro consta de 22 capítulos que tratan los diferentes aspectos gramaticales, y presenta sus reglas y usos de manera descriptiva y ejemplificada, con cuadros y esquemas que facilitan su comprensión.

En la primera parte del libro planteamos el estudio del sistema verbal: la formación de todos los modos y tiempos (tanto regulares como irregulares), de las perífrasis y de la voz pasiva, así como su uso.

En la segunda parte tratamos el sistema nominal: artículo, sustantivo, adjetivo, pronombre..., y se explican también las reglas de formación y uso.

El último apartado lo destinamos a las reglas básicas de ortografía y acentuación, áquellas con las que el aprendiz va a enfrentarse desde sus primeros contactos con la producción escrita.

Los autores

IDIOMAS HOY

Breve gramática

ESPAÑOL

LENGUA EXTRANJERA

de

Pedro Benítez
(Universidad de Alcalá de Henares)
y María José Gelabert

DIFUSION

Centro de Investigación y Publicaciones de Idiomas
C/ Bruch, 21. 1º-1ª
08010 Barcelona

Serie *IDIOMAS HOY*

Dirección editorial:
Detlev Wagner y Neus Sans

Coordinación editorial:
Olga Juan y Mireia Boadella

Breve gramática
ESPAÑOL LENGUA EXTRANJERA
de
Pedro Benítez (Universidad de Alcalá de Henares)
y María José Gelabert

Redacción Olga Juan

ISBN: 84-87099-75-0
Depósito legal: M-14596-1994
Printed in Spain
Gráficas Rama, S.A.

SER – ESTAR – HABER

	SER	**ESTAR**	**HABER**
Yo	soy	estoy	
Tú	eres	estás	
Él/ella/usted	es	está	hay
Nosotros/as	somos	estamos	
Vosotros/as	sois	estáis	
Ellos/as/ustedes	son	están	

USOS DE SER

❏ Para identificar/ identificarse:
- **Soy** Manolo. Mi nombre **es** Manolo López.
- ¿Quién **es** la profesora?
- ¿Qué **es** eso?
- París **es** una ciudad muy bonita.

❏ Para expresar la profesión: **ser** + *sustantivo*
- ¿**Eres** abogado?
- Yo **soy** electricista.

❏ Para expresar parentesco: **ser** + *sustantivo*
- Pedro y yo **somos** primos.

❏ Para expresar la nacionalidad u origen:
> **ser** + *adjetivo*
> **ser** + **de** + *nombre del país /ciudad*
- Fernando **es** alemán.
- Montserrat y yo **somos de** Barcelona.
- Ellos **son de** Bélgica.

❏ Para expresar materia: **ser** + **de** + *sustantivo*
- La mesa del comedor **es de** madera.
- Tu reloj **es de** oro.
- La copa **es de** cristal.

❏ Para expresar tiempo:
- ¿Qué hora **es**?
- ○ **Son** las tres.

- ¿Qué día **es**?
- ○ Hoy **es** lunes. / Hoy **es** 7 de mayo.

❑ Para expresar el precio:
- • ¿Cuánto **es?**
- ◦ **Son** dos mil seiscientas pesetas.

❑ Para expresar religión o idea política:
- • ¿De qué partido **eres?**
- ◦ **Soy** socialista/demócrata/...
- • Nosotros **somos** católicos/protestantes/...

❑ Para expresar características inherentes al sujeto: **ser** + *adjetivo*
- • Mi tío **es** gordo.
- • Estas chicas **son** altísimas.

❑ Para expresar apreciaciones subjetivas sobre informaciones o sucesos:
- • **Es** extraño que no haya llegado.
- • **Es** imposible vivir aquí.
- • **Es** bueno hacer deporte.

❑ Frases de pasiva: **ser** + *participio*
- • Cervantes **es** conocido por todos.

❑ Para valorar una actividad o período:
- • ¿Qué tal las vacaciones?
- ◦ Muy bien, **ha sido** una semana fenomenal.

❑ Con el sentido de "ocurrir /tener lugar":
- • El concierto **es** en la sala 5.
- • La fiesta **es** en mi casa.

USOS DE ESTAR

❑ Para expresar situación:
- • ¿Dónde **está** la catedral?
- ◦ **Está** al final de la calle.

- • ¿**Está** tu padre?
- ◦ No, **está** en la oficina.

- • **Estamos** a finales de octubre.

❑ Para expresar el estado físico: **estar bien/mal/**...
- • ¿Cómo **estáis?**
- ◦ **Estamos** bien, ¿y vosotros?

❑ Para expresar una actividad profesional: **estar** + **de** + *sustantivo*
- • Ahora **está de** camarero.

❏ Para expresar/describir algo temporal:

estar + *adjetivo*

- Últimamente come demasiado. **Está** gordísimo.
- ¡Qué antipático **está** estos días! ¿Sabes qué le pasa?
- Las manzanas **están** verdes.

estar + *gerundio*

- **Estamos** jugando a las cartas.
- ¡Chsss! La niña **está** durmiendo.

❏ Algunos adjetivos cambian de significado según vayan acompañados del verbo **ser** o del verbo **estar**:

ser malo	(travieso)	**estar** malo	(enfermo)
ser listo	(astuto)	**estar** listo	(preparado)
ser bueno	(bondadoso)	**estar** bueno	(sano)
ser atento	(cortés)	**estar** atento	(poner atención)
ser viejo	(anciano/añejo)	**estar** viejo	(estropeado/pasado)
ser verde	(color verde/joven/ obsceno)	**estar** verde	(inmaduro)
ser moreno	(piel oscura)	**estar** moreno	(bronceado)

USOS DE HAY

Es la forma impersonal del presente de indicativo del verbo **haber**.

Sirve tanto para el singular como para el plural:

- En la nevera **hay** una cerveza.
- **Hay** muchas casas en esta zona.

❏ Expresa la existencia de algo o de alguien:

- **Hay** coches en el garaje.
- **Hay** un estudiante inglés en la clase.

CONTRASTE ESTÁ- N/ HAY

Cuando se habla de algo que se presupone conocido por los hablantes se usa **estar**. Cuando no, se usa **hay**:

- ¿Dónde **está** el banco de Santander?
- Los zapatos **están** en el armario.

- ¿**Hay** una farmacia por aquí?
- **Hay** muchos estudiantes en la clase.

EL SISTEMA VERBAL

Hay tres grupos de verbos que se clasifican según la terminación:

1. grupo de verbos que terminan en **-ar** (cant**ar**)
2. grupo de verbos que terminan en **-er** (com**er**)
3. grupo de verbos que terminan en **-ir** (viv**ir**)

MODO INDICATIVO

El hablante se expresa de forma objetiva y da informaciones nuevas.

PRESENTE

REGULAR

	CANTAR	COMER	VIVIR
Yo	cant**o**	com**o**	viv**o**
Tú	cant**as**	com**es**	viv**es**
Él/ella/usted	cant**a**	com**e**	viv**e**
Nosotros/as	cant**amos**	com**emos**	viv**imos**
Vosotros/as	cant**áis**	com**éis**	viv**ís**
Ellos/as/ustedes	cant**an**	com**en**	viv**en**

IRREGULAR

1. Verbos con irregularidades propias:

ESTAR	DAR	SER	HABER	IR	SABER	CABER
estoy	doy	soy	he	voy	sé	quepo
estás	das	eres	has	vas	sabes	cabes
está	da	es	ha	va	sabe	cabe
estamos	damos	somos	hemos	vamos	sabemos	cabemos
estáis	dais	sois	habéis	vais	sabéis	cabéis
están	dan	son	han	van	saben	caben

2. Verbos que cambian la **-e-** de la raíz en **-ie-** en las tres personas del singular y la tercera persona del plural:

PENSAR	PERDER	PREFERIR
p**ie**nso	p**ie**rdo	pref**ie**ro
p**ie**nsas	p**ie**rdes	pref**ie**res
p**ie**nsa	p**ie**rde	pref**ie**re
pensamos	perdemos	preferimos
pensáis	perdéis	preferís
p**ie**nsan	p**ie**rden	pref**ie**ren

Otros verbos:

empezar, atravesar, calentar, cerrar, comenzar, despertar, divertir(se), encender, entender, fregar, gobernar, hervir, manifestar, mentir, merendar, negar, querer, recomendar, regar, sentar(se), sentir(se), sugerir, tener, venir...

3. Verbos que cambian la **-o-** de la raíz en **-ue-** en las tres personas del singular y la tercera del plural:

CONTAR	VOLVER	DORMIR
cuento	vuelvo	duermo
cuentas	vuelves	duermes
cuenta	vuelve	duerme
contamos	volvemos	dormimos
contáis	volvéis	dormís
cuentan	vuelven	duermen

Otros verbos:

acordar(se), acostar(se), almorzar, aprobar, avergonzar(se), cocer, colgar, costar, morir, mostrar, morder, mover, oler, poder, probar, recordar, resolver, rogar, soler, soñar, tostar, volar...

4. Verbos que cambian la **-e-** de la raíz en **-i-** en las tres personas del singular y la tercera del plural:

VESTIR
visto
vistes
viste
vestimos
vestís
visten

Otros verbos:

competir, corregir, decir, elegir, freír, medir, pedir, reír, repetir, seguir, servir...

5. Verbos que añaden una **-g-** en la primera persona del singular:

tener	tengo (**tienes**...)
poner	pongo (pones ...)
salir	salgo (sales...)
venir	vengo (**vienes**...)
decir	digo (dices...)
caer	caigo (caes...)
oír	oigo (**oyes**...)
valer	valgo (vales...)
traer	traigo (traes...)

6. Verbos terminados en **-acer, -ecer, -ocer, -ucir** añaden una **-z-** antes de la **-c-** en la primera persona del singular siendo las demás personas regulares:

nacer	nazco
merecer	merezco
parecer	parezco
pertenecer	pertenezco
agradecer	agradezco
conocer	conozco
traducir	traduzco
conducir...........................	conduzco
producir	produzco
reducir..............................	reduzco

EXCEPCIONES:

hacer	**hago** (haces...)
satisfacer..........................	**satisfago** (satisfaces...)
cocer	**cuezo** (cueces...)

7. Verbos terminados en **-uir,** convierten la **-i-** en **-y-** cuando aquélla se encuentra entre dos vocales:

HUIR
huyo
huyes
huye
huimos
huis
huyen

Otros verbos:
construir, destruir, concluir, disminuir, influir...

USOS DEL PRESENTE

❏ Para expresar acciones actuales:
> • Ahora **estudio** en la Universidad de Alcalá.

❏ Para expresar acciones habituales o frecuentes:
> • Siempre **bebo** vino en las comidas.

❏ Para expresar acciones futuras:
> • La semana próxima **salgo** de viaje.

❏ Para expresar acciones históricas/pasadas:
> • La Guerra Civil española **empieza** en 1936.

PRETÉRITO IMPERFECTO

REGULAR

	CANTAR	COMER	VIVIR
Yo	cantaba	comía	vivía
Tú	cantabas	comías	vivías
Él/ella/usted	cantaba	comía	vivía
Nosotros/as	cantábamos	comíamos	vivíamos
Vosotros/as	cantabais	comíais	vivíais
Ellos/as/ustedes	cantaban	comían	vivían

IRREGULAR

VER	SER	IR
veía	era	iba
veías	eras	ibas
veía	era	iba
veíamos	éramos	íbamos
veíais	erais	ibais
veían	eran	iban

USOS DEL PRETÉRITO IMPERFECTO

❏ Para expresar acciones habituales en el pasado, con frecuencia acompañado de marcadores temporales como: **generalmente, habitualmente, frecuentemente, siempre, todos los días**...

• Todos los días **comía** a la misma hora.

❏ Para describir situaciones/acciones del pasado:

• Mi abuela **era** alta y delgada. **Tenía** el pelo blanco…
• El edificio **era** tan alto que desde arriba **parecía** que la tierra se **movía**.

❏ Para describir acciones paralelas en desarrollo:

• Mis padres **preparaban** la cena mientras nosotros **poníamos** la mesa.

❏ Para referirse a la hora/ fecha/ estaciones del año o etapas de la vida:

• **Eran** las seis de la mañana cuando salí de casa.

❏ Para pedir algo de forma cortés:

• **Quería** ver el bolso del escaparate.

PRETÉRITO INDEFINIDO

REGULAR

	HABLAR	BEBER	VIVIR
Yo	hablé	bebí	viví
Tú	hablaste	bebiste	viviste
Él/ella/usted	habló	bebió	vivió
Nosotros/as	hablamos	bebimos	vivimos
Vosotros/as	hablasteis	bebisteis	vivisteis
Ellos/as/ustedes	hablaron	bebieron	vivieron

IRREGULAR

1. Los verbos terminados en **-ir** que en el *presente de indicativo* cambian la -**e**- de la raíz en **-ie-** y la **-e-** en **-i-,** en el *pretérito indefinido* cambian la -**e**- en **-i-** en la tercera persona del singular y del plural:

PREFERIR (Presente=prefiero)	PEDIR (Presente =pido)
preferí	pedí
preferiste	pediste
prefirió	pidió
preferimos	pedimos
preferisteis	pedisteis
prefirieron	pidieron

2. Los verbos terminados en **-ir** que en el *presente de indicativo* cambian la -**o**- de la raíz en **-ue-,** en el *pretérito indefinido* cambian la **-o-** en **-u-** en la tercera persona del singular y del plural:

DORMIR (Presente=duermo)
dormí
dormiste
durmió
dormimos
dormisteis
durmieron

3. Los verbos terminados en **-uir** que en el *presente de indicativo* cambian la **-i-** de la raíz en **-y-,** en el *pretérito indefinido* cambian la **-i-** en **-y-** en la tercera persona del singular y del plural:

CONSTRUIR (Presente= construyo)
construí
construiste
construyó
construimos
construisteis
construyeron

Los verbos **creer-leer-caer-oír** en el tiempo de pretérito indefinido se conjugan como **construir**.

4. Otros verbos irregulares:

tener	-	tuv		
saber	-	sup		-e
caber	-	cup		-iste
poder	-	pud	+	-o
poner	-	pus		-imos
haber	-	hub		-isteis
estar	-	estuv		-ieron
andar	-	anduv		

				-e
hacer	-	hic (**hizo**)		-iste
querer	-	quis	+	-o
venir	-	vin		-imos
				-isteis
				-ieron

decir	-	dij		-e
traer	-	traj		-iste
			+	-o
VERBOS EN -UCIR				-imos
conducir -		conduj		-isteis
				-eron

SER IR *	**DAR**
fui	di
fuiste	diste
fue	dio
fuimos	dimos
fuisteis	disteis
fueron	dieron

*La conjugación es igual pero se diferencian fácilmente por el contexto.

USOS DEL PRETÉRITO INDEFINIDO

Este tiempo puede ir acompañado de marcadores temporales que indican el inicio, el fin o la duración de la acción: **ayer, la semana pasada, el otro día, el mes/año pasado, en marzo, en 1989, muchas/varias veces, en seis /..../ocasiones, dos /... /días**...

- **El otro día** estuve en casa de Luis.
- Hizo **varias veces** ese viaje.
- Llegamos **en 1990**.

❏ Para expresar acciones del pasado, no relacionadas con el momento presente:
- Ayer **fui** al cine.

❏ Para expresar acciones acabadas de desarrollo rápido, momentáneo:
- **Apagó** la luz y **cerró** la puerta.

❏ Para expresar acciones de desarrollo prolongado, pero limitado y cerrado:
- **Estuve** dos años en México.
- El curso **duró** seis meses.

❏ Para describir acciones que se han repetido en el pasado:
- ¿Tu hermano **fue** varias veces a Madrid?
- En dos semanas **tomé** diez aviones.

❏ Para indicar una acción única que interrumpe a otra en su desarrollo:
- Estábamos cenando cuando **llegó** la policía.

FUTURO IMPERFECTO

REGULAR

Se forma con el *infinitivo* más las terminaciones propias del *futuro*.

Yo			-é
Tú	cantar		-ás
Él/ella/usted	comer	+	-á
Nosotros/as	vivir		-emos
Vosotros/as			-éis
Ellos/as/ustedes			-án

IRREGULAR

1. Verbos de raíz irregular:

			-é
			-ás
decir -	**dir**	+	-á
hacer -	**har**		-emos
			-éis
			-án

2. Grupo de verbos que pierden la vocal de la terminación del infinitivo:

saber -	**sabr**		-é
haber -	**habr**		-ás
caber -	**cabr**	+	-á
poder -	**podr**		-emos
querer -	**querr**		-éis
			-án

14

3. Grupo de verbos que cambian la vocal del infinitivo en **-d-**:

poner -	**pondr**		-é
tener -	**tendr**		-ás
salir -	**saldr**	+	-á
valer -	**valdr**		-emos
venir -	**vendr**		-éis
			-án

USOS DEL FUTURO IMPERFECTO

❏ Para expresar una acción futura, frecuentemente acompañado con expresiones de tiempo: **luego/ después, mañana (por la mañana/ tarde/ noche), la semana/ el mes/ el año que viene (próximo)**:

   • Luego **iré** de compras con mi madre.

❏ Para expresar probabilidad en el momento presente:

   • **Tendrá** 45 años, ¿no?

CONDICIONAL SIMPLE

REGULAR

Se forma con el *infinitivo* más las terminaciones propias del *condicional:*

Yo			-ía
Tú	cantar		-ías
Él/ella/usted	comer	+	-ía
Nosotros/as	vivir		-íamos
Vosotros/as			-íais
Ellos/as/ustedes			-ían

IRREGULAR

1. Verbos de raíz irregular:

		-ía
		-ías
decir - **dir**	+	-ía
hacer - **har**		-íamos
		-íais
		-ían

2. Grupo de verbos que pierden la vocal de la terminación del infinitivo:

saber	-	**sabr**	-ía
haber	-	**habr**	-ías
caber	-	**cabr** +	-ía
poder	-	**podr**	-íamos
querer	-	**querr**	-ían
			-ían

3. Grupo de verbos que cambian la vocal del infinitivo en **-d-**:

poner	-	**pondr**	-ía
tener	-	**tendr**	-ías
salir	-	**saldr** +	-ía
valer	-	**valdr**	-íamos
venir	-	**vendr**	-íais
			-ían

USOS DEL CONDICIONAL SIMPLE

❏ Para expresar probabilidad de una acción pasada:
   • Cuando llegamos **serían** las cinco de la tarde.

❏ Para expresar una acción cuya realización depende de una condición:
   • Si me lo explicaras, té **podría** ayudar.

❏ Para expresar deseo:
   • Me **bebería** una copa de cava.

❏ Para formular preguntas cortésmente, dar consejos o sugerencias:
   • ¿**Podrías** ayudarme?
   • Yo **iría** en tren, creo que es mejor.

PRETÉRITO PERFECTO

Se forma con el *presente de indicativo* del verbo **haber** más el *participio pasado* del verbo correspondiente.

Yo	he		
Tú	has		hablado
Él /ella/usted	ha	+	bebido
Nosotros/as	hemos		salido
Vosotros /as	habéis		
Ellos/as/ustedes	han		

USOS DEL PRETÉRITO PERFECTO

El pretérito perfecto puede ir acompañado de marcadores temporales: **este mes/año/...**, **esta mañana/semana/...**, **nunca, en mi vida**...

- **Esta semana** no han venido a verme.
- No lo he visto **en mi vida.**

❏ Para referirnos a una acción pasada relacionada con el presente:
- Esta semana **he ido** dos veces al teatro.
- **He trabajado** en esta empresa.

❏ Para referirnos a una acción no realizada incluyendo el presente:
- Nunca **hemos estado** en Mallorca.

❏ Para preguntar sobre la realización o no de un hecho:
- ¿**Has estado** alguna vez en San Pedro de Ribas?

❏ Para referirnos a acciones pasadas experimentadas, pero sin expresar el momento en el que se han realizado:
- Enrique **ha estado** en Barcelona muchas veces.

PRETÉRITO PLUSCUAMPERFECTO

Se forma con el *imperfecto* del verbo **haber** más el *participio pasado* del verbo correspondiente.

Yo	había		
Tú	habías		hablado
Él /ella/usted	había	+	bebido
Nosotros/as	habíamos		salido
Vosotros /as	habíais		
Ellos/as/ustedes	habían		

USOS DEL PRETÉRITO PLUSCUAMPERFECTO

❏ Para expresar acciones pasadas anteriores a otra acción pasada también:
- Cuando Juan llegó, yo **había salido.**
- Cuando entró en el cine, la película **había empezado.**

PRETÉRITO ANTERIOR

Se forma con el *indefinido* del verbo **haber** más el *participio pasado* del verbo que se conjuga.

Yo	hube		
Tú	hubiste		hablado
Él /ella/usted	hubo	+	bebido
Nosotros/as	hubimos		salido
Vosotros /as	hubisteis		
Ellos/as/ustedes	hubieron		

USOS DEL PRETÉRITO ANTERIOR

El uso de este tiempo es poco frecuente y generalmente se puede sustituir por el *pretérito indefinido* o el *pretérito pluscuamperfecto* de indicativo.

> • No se marchó hasta que **terminó/ había terminado** todo su trabajo.

❑ Expresa acciones pasadas anteriores a otras acciones pasadas también:

> • No se marchó hasta que **hubo terminado** todo su trabajo.

FUTURO PERFECTO

Se forma con el *futuro* del verbo **haber** más el *participio pasado* del verbo que se conjuga.

Yo	habré	
Tú	habrás	hablado
Él /ella/usted	habrá +	bebido
Nosotros/as	habremos	salido
Vosotros /as	habréis	
Ellos/as/ustedes	habrán	

USOS DEL FUTURO PERFECTO

❑ Para expresar acciones futuras que se realizan con anterioridad a otra acción futura también:

> • No lo veré porque cuando yo llegue él **habrá salido.**

❑ Para expresar probabilidad en el pasado:

> • No sé dónde está, me lo **habré dejado** en la oficina.

CONDICIONAL COMPUESTO

Se forma con el *condicional* del verbo **haber** más el *participio* pasado del verbo que se conjuga.

Yo	habría	
Tú	habrías	hablado
Él /ella/usted	habría +	bebido
Nosotros/as	habríamos	salido
Vosotros /as	habríais	
Ellos/as/ustedes	habrían	

USOS DEL CONDICIONAL COMPUESTO

❑ Para expresar probabilidad de un hecho anterior a una acción pasada:

> • ¿Por qué no **irían** a la fiesta?
> ○ Porque **habrían** estado discutiendo toda la tarde, ¿no?

IMPERATIVO

IMPERATIVO AFIRMATIVO

REGULAR

Las personas con las que se usa el *imperativo* son **tú, vosotros/-as y usted/-es.**

	HABLAR	COMER	ESCRIBIR
Tú	habla	come	escribe
Usted	hable	coma	escriba
Vosotros	hablad	comed	escribid
Ustedes	hablen	coman	escriban

IRREGULAR

1. La segunda persona del singular **tú** tiene las mismas irregularidades que el *presente de indicativo:*

	Presente de indicativo	**Imperativo**
Tú	empiezas	empieza
Tú	pides	pide
Tú	vuelves	vuelve
Tú	construyes	construye

Irregularidades propias del imperativo para **tú:**

salir	-	**sal**
tener	-	**ten**
poner	-	**pon**
venir	-	**ven**
hacer	-	**haz**
decir	-	**di**
ir	-	**ve**

2. La segunda persona del plural **vosotros** siempre es regular y se forma cambiando la **-r** del *infinitivo* por **-d:**

   - ¡**Empezad** a trabajar!
   - ¡**Volved** a casa!

3. Para **usted/-es** se usan las formas de la tercera persona singular y plural del *presente de subjuntivo:* *

Presente de subjuntivo (él/ellos)	Imperativo (usted/-es)
salga/ -n	salga/ -n
tenga/ -n	tenga/ -n
ponga/ -n	ponga/ -n
venga/ -n	venga/ -n
haga/ -n	haga/ -n
diga/ -n	diga/ -n
vaya/ -n	vaya/ -n

* Ver "Presente de subjuntivo"

19

IMPERATIVO + PRONOMBRE

La forma de *imperativo afirmativo* va seguida del pronombre personal complemento y forma una sola palabra.

- Dime
- Dímelo

En la segunda persona plural **vosotros** con verbos reflexivos la **-d** delante del pronombre personal **os** se pierde.

- Lavados — **Lavaos**
- Bebedos — **Bebeos**

IMPERATIVO NEGATIVO

Se usan las formas del *presente de subjuntivo* en negativo.

	HABLAR	COMER/ESCRIBIR
Tú	no hables	no comas/escribas
Usted	no hable	no coma/escriba
Vosotros/as	no habléis	no comáis/escribáis
Ustedes	no hablen	no coman/escriban

El *imperativo negativo* tiene, por tanto, las mismas irregularidades que el *presente de subjuntivo*:

	Presente de subjuntivo	Imperativo negativo
Tú	empieces	no empieces
Tú	pidas	no pidas
Tú	vuelvas	no vuelvas
Tú	huyas	no huyas

IMPERATIVO + PRONOMBRE

Los pronombres personales complemento preceden al verbo.

- No **lo** pongas aquí.
- No **me lo** compres todavía.

USOS DEL IMPERATIVO

❏ Para conceder permiso. Generalmente en la concesión del permiso repetimos el imperativo:

- ¿Puedo abrir la ventana?
- ○ Sí, **ábrela, ábrela.**

❏ Para dar instrucciones:

- **Siga** recto y en la tercera calle **gire** a la derecha.
- **Apriete** el botón y luego **abra** la tapa superior.

❏ Para dar consejo:

- **Salid** temprano, hay mucho tráfico.
- **No te pongas** las botas, hace mucho calor.

❏ Para ofrecer algo:

- **Toma** otra copa, todavía es temprano.
- **Coge** uno, están muy buenos.

❏ Para dar órdenes:

- **Ponte** la camisa blanca.
- **No salgas** antes de las siete.

MODO SUBJUNTIVO

El hablante participa subjetivamente en el enunciado que expresa y no da informaciones nuevas.

PRESENTE

REGULAR

	CANTAR	COMER	VIVIR
Yo	cante	coma	viva
Tú	cantes	comas	vivas
Él/ella/ustded	cante	coma	viva
Nosotros/as	cantemos	comamos	vivamos
Vosotros/as	cantéis	comáis	viváis
Ellos/as/ustedes	canten	coman	vivan

IRREGULAR

1. Verbos con irregularidades propias:

ESTAR	DAR	SER	HABER	IR	SABER
esté	dé	sea	haya	vaya	sepa
estés	des	seas	hayas	vayas	sepas
esté	dé	sea	haya	vaya	sepa
estemos	demos	seamos	hayamos	vayamos	sepamos
estéis	deis	seáis	hayáis	vayáis	sepáis
estén	den	sean	hayan	vayan	sepan

2. Verbos que cambian la **-e-** de la raíz en **-ie-** y la **-o-** en **-ue-** en las tres personas del singular y la tercera del plural en el *presente de indicativo* tienen en el *presente de subjuntivo* la misma irregularidad:

	PENSAR	VOLVER
	piense	vuelva
	pienses	vuelvas
	piense	vuelva
	pensemos	volvamos
	penséis	volváis
	piensen	vuelvan

Todos los verbos en **-ir** que en el *presente de indicativo* cambian la **-e-** en **-ie-** o la **-e-** en **-i-**, en el *presente de subjuntivo* tienen la misma irregularidad en las mismas personas y cambian la **-e-** en **-i-** en la primera y segunda persona del plural:

PREFER**IR**	PED**IR**
prefiera	pida
prefieras	pidas
prefiera	pida
prefiramos	pidamos
prefiráis	pidáis
prefieran	pidan

3. Los verbos **dormir** y **morir** cambian la **-o-** en **-u-** en la primera y segunda persona plural, las otras personas mantienen la misma irregularidad que en el *presente de indicativo:*

DORM**IR**	MOR**IR**
duerma	muera
duermas	mueras
duerma	muera
durmamos	muramos
durmáis	muráis
duerman	mueran

4. Los verbos que en el *presente de indicativo* tienen la primera persona irregular, presentan la misma irregularidad en todas las personas del *presente de subjuntivo:*

TE**NER**	CONO**CER**	CA**BER**
tenga	conozca	quepa
tengas	conozcas	quepas
tenga	conozca	quepa
tengamos	conozcamos	quepamos
tengáis	conozcáis	quepáis
tengan	conozcan	quepan

Otros verbos:
poner, salir, venir, decir, caer, nacer, merecer, parecer, producir...

5. Los verbos en **-uir** que en el *presente de indicativo* cambian la **-i-** en **-y-**, en el *presente de subjuntivo* tienen la misma irregularidad en todas las personas:

CONST**RUIR**
construya
construyas
construya
construyamos
construyáis
construyan

PRETÉRITO IMPERFECTO

REGULAR

	CANTAR	COMER	VIVIR
Yo	cantara/-ase	comiera/-iese	viviera/-iese
Tú	cantaras/-ases	comieras/-ieses	vivieras/-iese
Él/ella/usted	cantara/-ase	comiera/-iese	viviera/-iese
Nosotros/as	cantáramos/-ásemos	comiéramos/-iésemos	viviéramos/-iésemos
Vosotros/as	cantarais/-aseis	comierais/-ieseis	vivierais/-ieseis
Ellos/as/ustedes	cantaran/-asen	comieran/-iesen	vivieran/-iesen

IRREGULAR

El *imperfecto de subjuntivo* toma sus irregularidades de la tercera persona plural del *pretérito indefinido de indicativo* y las sigue en todas las personas.

Ejemplo con **tener**:
Tercera persona plural del *pretérito indefinido:* **tuvieron**.

	Pretérito imperfecto de subjuntivo	
Yo	tuviera	o tuviese
Tú	tuvieras	o tuvieses
Él/ella/usted	tuviera	o tuviese
Nosotros/as	tuviéramos	o tuviésemos
Vosotros/as	tuvierais	o tuvieseis
Ellos/as/ustedes	tuvieran	o tuviesen

Otros verbos:

Infinitivo	Pretérito indefinido 3ª persona plural	Pretérito imperfecto de subjuntivo 1ª persona singular	
ser	fueron	fuera	o fuese
ir	fueron	fuera	o fuese
estar	estuvieron	estuviera	o estuviese
tener	tuvieron	tuviera	o tuviese
hacer	hicieron	hiciera	o hiciese
decir	dijeron	dijera	o dijese
venir	vinieron	viniera	o viniese
poder	pudieron	pudiera	o pudiese
andar	anduvieron	anduviera	o anduviese
poner	pusieron	pusiera	o pusiese

PRETÉRITO PERFECTO

Se forma con el *presente de subjuntivo* del verbo **haber** más el *participio pasado* del verbo correspondiente.

Yo	haya	
Tú	hayas	
Él/ella/usted	haya	cantado
Nosotros/as	hayamos +	comido
Vosotros/as	hayáis	vivido
Ellos/as/ustedes	hayan	

PRETÉRITO PLUSCUAMPERFECTO

Se forma con el *pretérito imperfecto de subjuntivo* del verbo **haber** más el *participio pasado* del verbo correspondiente.

Yo	hubiera	o	hubiese	
Tú	hubieras	o	hubieses	
Él/ella/usted	hubiera	o	hubiese	cantado
Nosotros/as	hubiéramos	o	hubiésemos +	comido
Vosotros/as	hubierais	o	hubieseis	vivido
Ellos/as/ustedes	hubieran	o	hubiesen	

USOS DEL SUBJUNTIVO

Los tiempos del subjuntivo se emplean casi siempre formando parte de oraciones subordinadas.

En algunas oraciones se tiene que emplear indicativo o subjuntivo dependiendo de la intención del hablante y del tiempo en el que éste sitúe la acción respecto al acto de habla.

❑ Con verbos que expresan deseo, mandato, ruego, consejo, permiso, prohibición, voluntad... como **desear, querer, exigir, aconsejar, prohibir, necesitar**...:

> *verbo en indicativo* + **que** + *verbo en subjuntivo*

- Te prohibo **que llegues** más tarde de las ocho.
- El revisor nos aconsejó **que** no nos **alejáramos** de nuestro equipaje.
- ¡No, no te dejo **que salgas** a la calle con esta lluvia!

❏ Con verbos que expresan emociones y sentimientos como **lamentar, sentir, gustar**...:

> *verbo en indicativo + **que** + verbo en subjuntivo*

- Lamento mucho **que** no **puedas** venir a tomar café.
- Nos gusta **que haga** buen tiempo para motar en bici.

❏ Con expresiones impersonales como **es necesario, es mejor, es lógico, más vale**...:

> *expresión impersonal + **que** + verbo en subjuntivo*

- Es mejor **que tomes** el avión a las 8.
- Era lógico **que llegara** tarde, venía en tren.

❏ Con verbos de percepción física o mental como **ver, oír, notar** u **observar** en *forma negativa*, se usa *subjuntivo* e *indicativo*:

> *verbo en forma **afirmativa*** + **que** + *verbo en **indicativo***

- Luis notó **que** le **estaba** mintiendo.
- Oyó **que** Alberto **entraba.**

> *verbo en forma **negativa*** + **que** + *verbo en **subjuntivo***
> + *verbo en **indicativo***

- Luis **no notó que** le **estuviera** mintiendo.
- Luis **no notó que** le **estaba** mintiendo.

- **No oyó que** Alberto **entrara.**
- **No oyó que** Alberto **entraba.**

❏ Con verbos de actividad mental como **pensar, recordar, creer** u **opinar** en *forma negativa*, se usa *subjuntivo*:

> *en forma **afirmativa** + **que** + verbo en **indicativo***
> *en forma **negativa** + **que** + verbo en **subjuntivo***

forma afirmativa → indicativo:

- Creo **que** ellos **quieren** salir esta noche.
- Recuerdo **que tenía** mucho interés en este tema.

forma negativa → subjuntivo:

- No creo **que** ellos **quieran** salir esta noche.
- No recuerdo **que tenga** mucho interés en este tema.

❑ Con expresiones como **ocurre, es evidente, es cierto, es verdad, está claro, es...**, en *forma negativa* se usa *subjuntivo*:

> expresión **afirmativa** + **que** + *verbo en* **indicativo**
> expresión **negativa** + **que** + *verbo en* **subjuntivo**

expresión afirmativa ➡ indicativo:

- **Es cierto que tiene** ganas de venir, pero no le dejan.

- ¿Por qué llegáis tan tarde?
- ○ **Es que** el autobús **ha tenido** una avería.

expresión negativa ➡ subjuntivo:

- **No es cierto que tenga** ganas de venir a la fiesta, a él le gusta más la tranquilidad.
- **No está claro que vayamos** a Suiza a esquiar, está demasiado lejos.

❑ Con partículas temporales como **cuando, cada vez que, en cuanto, hasta que...**, se usa *subjuntivo* con frases que enuncian *acciones futuras*:

> acciones en *presente* o *pasado* ➡ *verbo en* **indicativo**
> acciones en *futuro* ➡ *verbo en* **subjuntivo**

presente o pasado ➡ indicativo:

- **Cuando** estoy cansado, **me acuesto** pronto.
- **En cuanto** llegó, me **llamó** por teléfono.

futuro ➡ subjuntivo:

- **Hasta que** no llame, no **me quedaré** tranquila.

¡Ojo! La partícula temporal **antes de que** *siempre* se usa con *subjuntivo*:

- Te lo digo **antes de que te enteres** por otra persona.

❑ Con partículas concesivas como **aunque, a pesar de que, por más que, por mucho que...**, se usa *subjuntivo* cuando el hablante presenta una acción que no es nueva, *sino presupuesta o compartida*:

> información nueva ➡ *verbo en* **indicativo**

- **Aunque llegó** tarde a clase, pudo entrar.
- **A pesar de que es** muy cabezón, a mí me hace caso.

> información presupuesta ➡ *verbo en* **subjuntivo**

- **Por mucho que** sea el hijo del jefe, tendrá que hacer el examen.
- **Aunque** me lo **hayan arreglado**, no funciona todavía.

❑ Con partículas finales como **para que**, **a fin de que**, **con (el fin de) que**..., *siempre* se usa *subjuntivo*:

• Te lo digo **para que** lo **sepas**.
• Iré a recogerte al aeropuerto **para que** no **cojas** un taxi.

❑ Con partículas condicionales como **en caso de que, a condición de que, con tal de que**..., *siempre* se usa *subjuntivo*:

• Te dejo el libro **con tal de que** me lo **devuelvas** mañana.
• **En caso de que** no **venga**, se lo mandas por correo.

❑ Con oraciones introducidas por un pronombre relativo: **que, quien, donde, cual, como**..., se usa *subjuntivo* cuando el *antecedente es desconocido* o *se presupone que existe*:

*el antecedente **existe** o es **conocido*** ➨ *verbo en* **indicativo**

• Busco a una chica **que tiene** los ojos azules.
• Encontré a Luis **donde** ayer te **encontré** a ti.

*el antecedente es **desconocido*** ➨ *verbo en* **subjuntivo**

• Quiero para el puesto a alguien **que hable** inglés.
• Me gustaría ir a un lugar **donde toquen** "blues".

❑ Con partículas que expresan hipótesis o probabilidad como **quizá(s), tal vez**..., se usa *subjuntivo* cuando el hablante lo enuncia con *duda* o *inseguridad*:

seguridad *del hablante* ➨ *verbo en* **indicativo**

• **Quizá viene** con su tío.

¡Ojo! **A lo mejor** *siempre* se usa con **indicativo**:

• **A lo mejor cambia** de opinión de aquí al fin de semana.

inseguridad *del hablante* ➨ *verbo en* **subjuntivo**

• **Tal vez venga** Luisa el fin de semana.
• **Quizá** me **cojan** de suplente en el colegio.

❑ Partícula **si** condicional.
-Condición real: se expresa seguridad en el cumplimiento de los hechos.

si + *presente de indicativo* **+** *indicativo*
               (presente, futuro o imperativo)

• **Si tengo** vacaciones me iré a la playa.

-Condición hipotética: se expresa hipótesis en el cumplimiento de los hechos.

> **si +** *imperfecto de subjuntivo* **+** *condicional simple*

- **Si tuviera** vacaciones me iría a la playa.

- Condición irreal: se expresa la imposibilidad del cumplimiento de los hechos.

> **si +** *pluscuamperfecto de subjuntivo* **+** *condicional compuesto*
> *o pluscuamperfecto de subjuntivo*

- **Si hubiera tenido** vacaciones me habría ido/**hubiera ido** a la playa.

FORMAS NO PERSONALES

INFINITIVO

Es una forma no personal del verbo.

El hablante lo usa para referirse a la noción verbal, sin dar ninguna información.

Puede funcionar como **sustantivo** y como **verbo.**

USOS DEL INFINITIVO

Como verbo:

Tiene foma simple y compuesta:

> **cantar/ haber cantado**

Voz activa y voz pasiva:

> **escribir/ ser escrito**

❑ Generalmente va en frases con uno o más verbos conjugados:

- Me gusta **beber** por las noches.
- Está preocupado por **aprender.**
- Tengo cinco libros para **leer**.
- Pensaba **quedarme** en casa este fin de semana.

❑ Forma el núcleo verbal de las perífrasis de infinitivo*:

- **Tengo que salir** pronto.
- **Debe de estar** en su casa.

Como sustantivo:

❑ Se puede sustantivar añadiendo cualquier determinante (artículo, demostrativo...). Toma el género masculino y el número singular o plural:

- **Su poder** es mucho en la empresa.
- **Los deberes** son muchos.

❑ También se puede sustantivar de forma impersonal:

- **Viajar** es divertido.

❑ Puede ir acompañado de adjetivos:

> el **buen comer**
> el **mucho hablar**

* Ver "La perífrasis con infinitivo"

❏ Algunos tienen una sustantivación permanente porque se usan con mucha frecuencia:

el deber	—	los deberes
el poder	—	los poderes
el ser	—	los seres

GERUNDIO

Es una forma no personal del verbo.

Tiene forma simple y compuesta:
cantando/habiendo cantado

Tiene forma activa y pasiva:
estudiando/siendo estudiado

Se forma:

REGULAR

Verbos terminados en **-ar**	→	**- ando**
Verbos terminados en **-er, -ir**	→	**-iendo**

IRREGULAR

1. Los verbos terminados en **-ir** que en *presente de indicativo* cambian la **-e-** de la raíz en **-ie-/-e-**, en *gerundio* cambian la **-e-** en **-i-**:

pedir	→	p**i**diendo	preferir	→	pref**i**riendo
vestir	→	v**i**stiendo	sentir	→	s**i**ntiendo

2. Los verbos **dormir**, **morir** y **poder** cambian la **-o-** de la raíz en **-u-**:

dormir	→	d**u**rmiendo
morir	→	m**u**riendo
poder	→	p**u**diendo

3. Si la raíz termina en *vocal*, se sustituye la terminación **-er, -ir** por **-yendo**:

Verbos terminados en **-uir**... hu**yendo**, constru**yendo**					
caer	→	ca**yendo**	traer	→	tra**yendo**
creer	→	cre**yendo**	leer	→	le**yendo**
oír	→	o**yendo**	ir	→	**yendo**

USOS DEL GERUNDIO

❏ Es una forma verbal que expresa duración que puede ser anterior, simultánea o posterior a la acción que expresa el verbo conjugado:

- **Hablando** por teléfono no puedes solucionarlo, tienes que ir personalmente.
- El avión cayó al mar, **muriendo** todos los pasajeros.
- **Saliendo** tarde he llegado pronto.

❏ Forma el núcleo verbal de las perífrasis de gerundio*:

- **Salió corriendo** como si llegara tarde.
- **Está estudiando** para los exámenes.

PARTICIPIO

Es una forma no personal del verbo que puede funcionar como verbo y como adjetivo. Concuerda en género y número con el sustantivo al que acompaña, excepto en la formación de los tiempos compuestos con el verbo **haber.** Se forma:

REGULAR

Verbos terminados en **-ar**	➞	**-ado**
Verbos terminados en **-er, -ir**	➞	**-ido**

IRREGULAR

hacer	➞	**hecho**	decir	➞	**dicho**
volver	➞	**vuelto**	poner	➞	**puesto**
abrir	➞	**abierto**	ver	➞	**visto**
escribir	➞	**escrito**	romper	➞	**roto**
resolver	➞	**resuelto**			

USOS DEL PARTICIPIO

Como verbo:

❏ Es el núcleo verbal de los tiempos compuestos:

haber + *participio*

- Esta mañana **hemos salido** pronto de casa.
- **He comido** en el restaurante de la esquina.

* Ver "La perífrasis con gerundio"

32

❑ Es el núcleo verbal de las formas pasivas:

> **ser** + *participio*
>
> - Aquella casa **fue construida** por Gaudí.
> - Estos libros **han sido escritos** por Miguel Delibes.

❑ Forma el núcleo verbal de las perífrasis de participio*:

> - Sólo **llevo leídas** cien páginas del libro.
> - El televisor ya **está arreglado.**

Como adjetivo:

❑ El participio puede emplearse en función de adjetivo y acompaña al nombre:

> - Mi hermano es una **persona** muy **decidida.**
> - ¡Qué **chicos** tan **divertidos**!

---

* Ver "La perífrasis con participio"

LA PERÍFRASIS

Verbo auxiliar	+	- que/preposición/Ø + **infinitivo**
el que se conjuga		- gerundio
		- preposición/Ø + **participio**

CON INFINITIVO

Expresan el principio de una acción proyectada hacia el futuro a partir del tiempo en que está el verbo auxiliar.

- Me **pongo a trabajar.**
- Me **pondré a trabajar.**
- Me **puse a trabajar.**

La totalidad del concepto verbal es de presente, pasado o futuro.

❑ **Ir a** + *infinitivo*

– Expresa la idea de posterioridad inmediata al tiempo en el que se sitúa la acción con una idea de intencionalidad.

- **Voy a comprar.**
- **Iba a comprar** y me encontré con Luis.

– Cuando el verbo **ir** va en futuro o imperativo recobra su propio sentido:

- **Ve** a estudiar.
- No **irás** a jugar con tus amigos; estás castigado.

❑ **Pasar a** + *infinitivo*

- Estos chicos **pasaron a formar** parte de mi equipo el año pasado.

❑ **Echar a** + *infinitivo*

- Cuando le vio, **echó a correr**.

❑ **Acabar de** + *infinitivo*

- **Acabo de enterarme** de algo muy curioso.

❑ **Ponerse a** + *infinitivo*

- En cuanto llega a casa **se pone a estudiar**.

❑ **Llegar a** + *infinitivo*

- En dos meses **llegó a adelgazar** 25 Kg.

❑ **Volver a** + *infinitivo*

- **No volveré a hacer**lo, es muy difícil.

❑ **Dejar de** + *infinitivo*

- Hace dos meses que **dejó de fumar**.

❑ **Acabar por** + *infinitivo*

- Discutían sin cesar y él **acabó por cambiarse** de habitación.

❑ **Soler** + *infinitivo*

- El director **suele llegar** a las nueve.

❑ **Tener que**
   Haber de + *infinitivo*

Para expresar la necesidad u obligación:

- **Tienes que estudiar** para el examen, ¿cómo quieres aprobar si no?
- **Hemos de salir** a las 8 y media para llegar bien.

❑ **Hay que** + *infinitivo*

Para expresar impersonalidad o para dar instrucciones sobre la realización de algo:

- **Hay que trabajar** para vivir.
- **Hay que encender** primero la impresora, luego **hay que poner** el papel y **dar** la orden. Ya está.

❑ **Deber (de)** + *infinitivo*

Para expresar la necesidad u obligación de manera subjetiva, a veces con carácter moral. En algunos casos **deber de** expresa probabilidad:

- **Debo visitarle**, hace mucho tiempo que no sé nada de él.
- **Deben de** ser las ocho de la tarde.

CON GERUNDIO

Expresan una acción durativa. Los matices significativos dependen del verbo que lo acompaña.

- **Sigue buscando** piso.

❏ **Estar** + *gerundio*

Se usa cuando nos interesa hacer hincapié en el desarrollo de una acción y para responder a la pregunta sobre el lugar en dónde se encuentra alguien.

- ¿Qué hace Luis?
- **Está estudiando.**

- ¿Y tus padres?
- **Están viajando** por Alemania.

❏ **Llevar** + *gerundio*

Expresa el desarrollo de una acción que comienza en el pasado.

- **Lleva** tres años **viviendo** en EE.UU.
  (= Hace tres años que vive en EE.UU.)

❏ **Ir** + *gerundio*

Se usa para destacar que el desarrollo de la acción se produce lentamente.

- ¿Cómo está tu madre?
- **Va mejorando.**

❏ **Andar** + *gerundio*

Se utiliza para añadir cierto valor despectivo al desarrollo de la acción.

- ¿Qué hace tu hermana?
- No sé.. **Anda buscando** trabajo.

CON PARTICIPIO

Expresan una acción perfectiva y marcan la fase final de la acción verbal. El participio concuerda con el objeto directo o el atributo.

- **Llevan vendidos** 58 libros de la colección.
- Sólo **llevan vendido** 1 libro de la colección.
- La casa **está** recién **construida.**

❏ **Ir** + *participio*

- **Van hechos** tres paquetes, sólo nos faltan cinco.

❏ **Traer** + *participio*

- Mira, **traen rotas** las camisas...

❏ **Tener** + *participio*

- Las **tenemos vendidas** todas, no queda ni una.

❏ **Dejar** + *participio*

  • Por la mañana, antes de salir, **dejo hecha** la comida.

❏ **Quedar** + *participio*

  • Cuando salen, **quedan abiertas** todas las puertas.

❏ **Dar por** + *participio*

  • Son las tres, **damos por terminada** la reunión.

LA VOZ PASIVA

Se forma:

> verbo **ser** + **participio** del verbo que se conjuga + (**por** + *sustantivo agente*)

- La casa **es construida por** los obreros.

El participio concuerda en género y número con el elemento que actúa como sujeto paciente.

- **Las casas son construidas por** los obreros.

La voz pasiva se utiliza poco en español.

PASIVA CON SE

Se forma:

> **se** + verbo en **3º persona del singular/plural** + *sustantivo*

- **Se alquila** piso.
- **Se venden** patatas gallegas.

El verbo concuerda en número con el sustantivo.

IMPERSONAL CON SE

Se forma:

> **se** + verbo en **3ª persona del singular** + *adverbio*

- **Se come bien** en ese restaurante.
- **Se lee poco** en España.

El **se** puede sustituirse por **gente, uno**:

- La **gente** bebe poco en este país.
- **Uno** come bien en ese restaurante.

EL ARTÍCULO

El artículo concuerda con el sustantivo en género y número.
Hay dos clases de artículos: el determinado y el indeterminado.

ARTÍCULOS DETERMINADOS

	masculino	femenino	neutro
singular	el	la	lo
plural	los	las	

El hablante emplea el artículo determinado cuando se refiere a un elemento
ya introducido en el discurso o que se presupone conocido.

USOS DE EL/LA/LOS/LAS

Los artículos determinados masculinos y femeninos se usan con:

❏ Sustantivo sujeto de la oración:

- ¿**La** ventana está cerrada?
- A mí me gusta **el** chocolate.
- ¿Dónde están **los** niños?

❏ Horas:

- Son **las** dos menos veinte.

❏ Sustantivo objeto directo de la oración cuando éste es específico:

- Juan y Luis compran **los** regalos de Navidad.
- ¿Escribes **las** cartas a máquina?

❏ Nombres no contables con carácter identificador:

- ¿Me puedes dar **el** azúcar?
- Oye, Antonio, saca **el** dinero del banco.

❏ Atributo (sustantivo), precedido por el verbo **ser**, con carácter
identificador:

- ¿Martín es **el** profesor?
- Mira, ese actor es **el** malo de la película.

❏ Tratamiento (señor/señora/señorita/marqués/ doctor/capitán/...), cuando se habla de esta persona sin estar presente o es desconocida:

- Me han dicho que **el** señor López es el director.
- Oiga, por favor, ¿es usted **el** doctor González?

❏ Apellido, cuando se habla de los miembros de la familia, se usa **los** + *apellido:*

- **Los González** se han comprado un piso nuevo.
- **Los Guardiola** vienen a comer.

❏ Nombres de las partes del cuerpo y objetos personales:

- Me duele **la** cabeza.
- ¿Dónde están **las** llaves?

❏ Nombres de ríos, montañas, mares y lagos:

- **El Tajo** desemboca en Lisboa.
- **Los Pirineos** están en el norte de España.

❏ Días de la semana/estaciones del año:

- La inauguración del curso es **el** martes.
- ¿La cosecha es en (**el**) verano?

USOS DEL ARTÍCULO NEUTRO LO

Es invariable.

❏ Se usa para sustantivar adjetivos, participios y oraciones adjetivas o de relativo:

- **Lo** mejor es llegar pronto.
- **Lo** firmado se tiene que cumplir.
- Explicó **lo** que creía importante.

Este artículo da al adjetivo un carácter abstracto.

OMISIÓN DEL ARTÍCULO DETERMINADO

Se omite el artículo determinado cuando:

❏ Acompaña a los nombres propios *(sujeto-objeto directo):*

- Luis es estudiante de arquitectura.
- Esta semana visitamos Barcelona.

❏ El objeto directo es genérico:

> • Siempre comen sardinas, les gustan mucho.
> • Yo nunca bebo cerveza.

❏ Los nombres no contables indican cantidades indeterminadas:

> • Oye, Antonio, saca dinero del banco. Sólo tengo mil pesetas.
> • ¿Me puedes dar azúcar, por favor?

❏ El atributo tiene carácter clasificador/genérico:

> • ¿Martín es profesor?
> • Ese actor es médico.

❏ El verbo **ser** va acompañado de los días de la semana y de las estaciones del año:

> • Hoy es miércoles.
> • ¡Ya es primavera!

❏ Se habla con una persona y utilizamos forma de tratamiento:

> • Señor López, ¿puede atenderme un momento?
> • Buenas tardes, doctor González.

ARTÍCULOS INDETERMINADOS

	masculino	femenino
singular	un	una
plural	unos	unas

El hablante emplea el artículo indeterminado cuando introduce un elemento nuevo en el discurso.

USOS DE UN/UNA/UNOS/UNAS

Los artículos indeterminados se usan con:

❏ Sustantivo sujeto de una oración:

> • **Una** secretaria tiene que saber idiomas.

❏ Sustantivo objeto directo:

> • Tengo **un** libro de Camilo José Cela.
> • Mi amiga Luisa tiene **unos** padres muy modernos.

❑ Un atributo +adjetivo, precedido del verbo **ser:**

- ¿Almodóvar es **un** director de cine?
- El que habla es **un** investigador polaco.

❑ Un atributo (sin adjetivo), precedido del verbo **ser:**

- ¿Quién es ?
- Emilia. Es **una** secretaria.

- ¿Y aquéllos?
- **Unos** arquitectos de la empresa.

OMISIÓN DEL ARTÍCULO INDETERMINADO

Se omite el artículo indeterminado cuando:

❑ Acompaña a un atributo, precedido del verbo **ser,** para clasificarlo:

- Almodóvar es director de cine.
- Es interesante. El que habla es investigador.
- Emilia es secretaria.
- Aquéllos son arquitectos de la empresa.

❑ Acompaña a los adjetivos **otro** y **cierto**:

- ¿No hay otro libro?

CASOS ESPECIALES DE CONCORDANCIA

Los sustantivos en femenino singular que empiezan por **a/ha** acentuada van acompañados de **el.** En plural mantienen la concordancia:

el agua — las aguas   **el ha**da — las hadas

Con el artículo indeterminado se puede usar **un** y **una**:

un hada — **una ha**da

ARTÍCULOS CONTRACTOS

de + el = **del**
a + el = **al**

Unión de las preposiciones **a** y **de** con el artículo **el:**

- Voy **al** cine.
- Regresamos **del** viaje.

EL NOMBRE O SUSTANTIVO

El nombre es una palabra variable en género y número.

GÉNERO DE LOS SUSTANTIVOS

SON SIEMPRE MASCULINOS:

❏ Las palabras que nombran seres de sexo masculino:

> el abogado, el hombre, el guardia, el albañil, el caballo...

❏ Los nombres de los días de la semana:

> el lunes, el martes, el miércoles, el jueves, el viernes, el sábado, el domingo.

❏ Los nombres de los meses del año:

> enero, febrero, marzo, abril, mayo, junio, julio, agosto, setiembre, octubre, noviembre, diciembre.

❏ La mayoría de los nombres de ríos, mares, océanos y lagos:

> el río Ebro, el mar Mediterráneo, el océano Atlántico, el lago de Sanabria...

❏ La mayoría de los nombres de sistemas montañosos:

> los Pirineos, los Andes, los Alpes...

a excepción de los que van acompañados de las palabras **cordillera** o **sierra**:

> la cordillera Ibérica, la sierra de Gata....

SUELEN SER MASCULINOS:

❏ Los sustantivos terminados en **-o**:

> **el** niño, **el** caballo, **el** vaso, **el** libro, **el** teléfono, **el** pájaro, **el** bolso.....

❏ Los que terminan en **-or**:

> **el** amor, **el** dolor, **el** color...

a excepción de: la flor, la labor.

❏ Los que terminan en **-aje**:

> **el** vi**aje**, **el** gar**aje**, **el** tr**aje**...

❏ La mayoría de los nombres de árboles:

> el pino, el manzano, el abeto, el naranjo, el limonero...

SON SIEMPRE FEMENINOS:

❏ Las palabras que nombran seres de sexo femenino:

> la profesora, la mujer, la madre, la vaca...

❏ Los nombres de letras del alfabeto:

> la a, la be, la ce, la de, la e, la efe, la ge, la hache...

SUELEN SER FEMENINOS:

❏ Los terminados en **-a**:

> **la** niñ**a**, **la** mes**a**, **la** sill**a**, **la** señor**a**, **la** botell**a**, **la** cop**a**, **la** bols**a**...

a excepción de los que se refieren a seres de sexo masculino:

> el policía, el taxista, el idiota, el belga...

y las palabras de origen griego que se refieren a seres inanimados:

> el problema, el planeta...

❏ Los terminados en **-dad** y en **-tad**:

> **la** solidari**dad**, **la** amis**tad**...

❏ Los terminados en **-ción, -sión, -zón**:

> **la** oposi**ción**, **la** pose**sión**, **la** ra**zón**...

a excepción de:

> el corazón, el buzón...

❏ Los terminados en **-ez**:

> **la** niñ**ez**, **la** vej**ez**, **la** estupid**ez**...

❏ Los terminados en **-tud**:

> **la** juven**tud**, **la** multi**tud**...

❏ Los terminados en **-dumbre**:

> **la** muche**dumbre**...

❏ La mayoría de los nombres de profesiones son masculinos, sin embargo es frecuente el empleo de dichas palabras en femenino:

el médico	–	**la** médic**a**
el ministro	–	**la** ministr**a**
el abogado	–	**la** abogad**a**

CAMBIOS DE SIGNIFICADO

el corte	–	la corte
el bolso	–	la bolsa
el capital	–	la capital
el policía	–	la policía
el guía	–	la guía
el cólera	–	la cólera

FORMACIÓN DEL FEMENINO

Generalmente el femenino se forma a partir del masculino:

❏ Se cambia la **-o** en **-a:**

gat**o**	–	gat**a**
niñ**o**	–	niñ**a**

❏ Se añade una **-a** a la palabra masculiná que termina en *consonante* (**-l, -or**):

chava**l**	–	chava**la**
profes**or**	–	profes**ora**

❏ Con los sufijos **-esa, -isa, -triz**:

alcalde	–	alcald**esa**
poeta	–	poet**isa**
actor	–	ac**triz**

FORMAS ESPECIALES

el hombre	–	la mujer
el rey	–	la reina
el padre	–	la madre
el yerno	–	la nuera
el macho	–	la hembra
el caballo	–	la yegua
el toro	–	la vaca
el gallo	–	la gallina

FORMACIÓN DEL PLURAL

Nombres terminados en:

❏ *Vocal* + **s:**

la cas**a**	–	las cas**as**
el men**ú**	–	los men**ús**

❏ *Consonante/***y/í** + es:

la pare**d**	–	las pare**des**
el re**y**	–	los re**yes**
el jabal**í**	–	los jabal**íes**

❏ **-z** cambia a **-ces:**

el pe**z**	–	los pe**ces**

❏ **-s** (monosílabos o nombres con acento en la última sílaba) + **es:**

el pa**ís**	–	los paí**ses**
el **gas**	–	los gas**es**

CASOS ESPECIALES

❏ Algunos nombres son iguales en singular que en plural:

la tesis	–	**las tesis**
el paraguas	–	**los paraguas**

❏ Algunos nombres sólo se usan en plural:

las gafas
las tijeras

❏ El plural masculino incluye el género masculino y femenino:

los padres
los tíos
los primos
los señores

EL ADJETIVO

CONCORDANCIA

El adjetivo concuerda en género y número con el sustantivo al que acompaña.

- Se ha comprado un vestido blanco.
- Tiene dos chaquetas amarillas.

Si el adjetivo se refiere a dos o más sustantivos y uno es masculino el adjetivo será masculino.

- La chaqueta, los pantalones y la camisa son negros.

FORMACIÓN DEL FEMENINO

❑ Los adjetivos que terminan en **-o** forman el femenino en **-a**:

bueno	–	buena
bonito	–	bonita

❑ Los que terminan en **-n** y en **-r** añaden una **-a**:

encantador	–	encantadora
holgazán	–	holgazana

❑ Los adjetivos de nacionalidad que terminan en *consonante* añaden una **-a**:

inglés	–	inglesa
alemán	–	alemana

❑ Los adjetivos que terminan en **-e** son invariables:

libre	–	libre
caliente	–	caliente

❑ Algunos adjetivos que terminan en *consonante* son invariables:

fácil	–	fácil
joven	–	joven

FORMACIÓN DEL PLURAL

El plural se forma añadiendo una -s cuando el adjetivo termina en *vocal:*

o .... -os
a .... -as
e .... -es

bueno .... buenos
rubia .... rubias
fuerte .... fuertes

y cuando termina en *consonante* se añade -es:

joven   –   jóvenes
fácil   –   fáciles

POSICIÓN DEL ADJETIVO

❑ Los adjetivos calificativos suelen ir detrás del sustantivo:

    • Los pantalones **azules** que te has comprado te quedan muy bien.

❑ Cuando los adjetivos van delante del sustantivo tienen matiz enfático:

    • Luis dibuja con **asombrosa** habilidad.

❑ Algunos adjetivos calificativos cambian su significado según se encuentren delante o detrás del sustantivo:

    • Regalo la ropa usada de mis hijos para los niños **pobres.**
    • **Pobres** niños, están sufriendo mucho.

❑ Hay adjetivos que pierden la -o final cuando van delante de un sustantivo masculino singular: **bueno, malo, primero, tercero, alguno, ninguno**...

    • Tiene la oficina en el **primer** piso y vive en el tercero.
    • ¿Hay **algún** libro de ese autor en la biblioteca?

SUSTANTIVACIÓN DEL ADJETIVO

El adjetivo masculino singular precedido por el artículo neutro **lo** puede formar sustantivos:

    lo bueno
    lo difícil
    lo interesante

LA COMPARACIÓN

COMPARACIÓN DE IGUALDAD

❏ **Tan** + *adjetivo/adverbio* + **como**:

> • Luisa es **tan** alta **como** yo.

❏ **Tanto/a/os/as** + *sustantivo* + **como**:

> • Mi hermano tiene **tantos** libros **como** Juan.

❏ *Verbo* + **tanto como** + *sustantivo:*

> • Estudia **tanto como** su amigo.

COMPARACIÓN DE DESIGUALDAD

Inferioridad

❏ **Menos** + *sustantivo/adjetivo* + **que**:

> • Tengo **menos** dinero **que** Manolo.
> • La película es **menos** interesante **que** el libro.

❏ *Verbo* + **menos que** + *sustantivo/verbo:*

> • Como **menos que** Luis.
> • Duerme **menos que** trabaja.

Superioridad

❏ **Más** + *sustantivo/adjetivo* + **que**:

> • Su hija es **más** estudiosa **que** la mía.
> • María tiene **más** discos **que** Gloria.

❏ *Verbo* + **más que** + *sustantivo/verbo:*

> • Paco bebe **más que** su mujer.
> • Paco bebe **más que** come.

COMPARATIVOS IRREGULARES

más bueno	—	**mejor**
más malo	—	**peor**
más pequeño	—	**menor**
más grande	—	**mayor**

El SUPERLATIVO

Relativo:

❑ **El/la/los/las más** + *adjetivo (de):*

- Este chico es **el más** listo de la clase.

Absoluto:

❑ *Adjetivo* **+-ísimo/a/os/as**:

- Aquel hotel es **carísimo**.

SUPERLATIVOS IRREGULARES

rico	—	**riquísimo**
antiguo	—	**antiquísimo**
fuerte	—	**fortísimo**
pobre	—	**paupérrimo**

LOS DEMOSTRATIVOS

Determinan al sustantivo tomando como punto de referencia la situación del hablante tanto en el espacio (**aquí, ahí, allí**) como en el tiempo (**cercanía ... lejanía**).

ADJETIVOS Y PRONOMBRES DEMOSTRATIVOS

	masculino	femenino	neutro (pronombre)
singular	este	esta	esto
	ese	esa	eso
	aquel	aquella	aquello
plural	estos	estas	
	esos	esas	
	aquellos	aquellas	

Relación espacial respecto del hablante:

aquí	este/ esta/ esto /...
ahí	ese / esa / eso /...
allí	aquel / aquella / aquello /...

Relación temporal respecto del hablante:

próximo:	este / esta / esto /...
	ese / esa / eso /...
lejos:	aquel / aquella / aquello /...

Los **demostrativos adjetivos** determinan al nombre y no llevan acento gráfico.

Suelen ir delante del sustantivo:

- Me gustan **aquellos** zapatos.
- Mira **ese** cuadro, es interesante.

Pero cuando el sustantivo va acompañado del artículo, el demostrativo va detrás:

- Los niños **esos** no estudian nada.

Los **demostrativos pronombres** sustituyen al nombre y suelen llevar acento gráfico.

- ¿Te gusta este jersey?
- Prefiero **ése**, el azul.

- Esos cuadros son bonitos pero **aquéllos** tienen un colorido fantástico.

Los demostrativos pronombres tienen formas neutras:

- ¿Qué es **eso**?
- ¿Cuánto cuesta **esto**?
- **Aquello** era imposible.

LOS POSESIVOS

Establecen una relación de pertenencia entre los objetos y las personas. Concuerdan en género y número con la cosa poseída.

ADJETIVOS Y PRONOMBRES POSESIVOS

UN POSEEDOR		
	adjetivo	pronombre
1º persona	mi/s	mío/a/os/as
2º persona	tu/s	tuyo/a/os/as
3º persona	su/s	suyo/a/os/as

DOS o MÁS POSEEDORES		
	adjetivo	pronombre
1º persona	nuestro/a/os/as	
2º persona	vuestro/a/os/as	
3º persona	su/s	suyo/a/os/as

- **Mis** amigos son australianos.
- **Nuestro** perro se llama Boby.

- ¿Es **tuyo** el paraguas ?
- No, no es **mío**.

- ¿**Vuestro** profesor es español?
- Sí, de Badajoz.

El **adjetivo/pronombre posesivo** concuerda en género y número con el nombre, no con la persona poseedora.

- Una amiga de Luis. → Es una amiga **suya** (= de Luis) no **mía**.
- Las casas de **mi** padre. → Estas casas son **suyas.**

Las formas de **pronombre** pueden ir acompañadas del artículo determinado **el/la/los/las**.

- Nuestro *coche* es más potente que **el vuestro**.
- Aunque llevo mis *llaves* no olvides **las tuyas**.
- Tu *hijo* es dos años mayor que **el mío**.

- ¿Conoces a Sebas?
- ○ Claro, si es amigo **mío.**

- ¿Sabes, los López? Pues un hijo **suyo** ha tenido un accidente y está en el hospital.

En otras lenguas se usa un posesivo cuando en español usamos un artículo determinado o un pronombre personal.

- Tengo que cortarme **el** pelo.
- Siempre lleva **los** ojos pintados.
- Me duele **la** cabeza.

Los **posesivos adjetivos** van delante del sustantivo:

- **Mi** amigo y **sus** padres se encontraron con **nuestros** abuelos en el parque.

Los posesivos se sitúan detrás del sustantivo cuando éste va acompañado de un determinante:

- Te presento a Juan, **un** compañero **mío.**

LOS PRONOMBRES PERSONALES

Sirven para referirse a las personas que intervienen en la conversación.

SUJETO

	singular	plural
1º persona	yo	nosotros/ -as
2º persona	tú	vosotros/ -as
3º persona	él/ella/usted	ellos/ -as/ustedes

Las formas **usted/ustedes** son segunda persona en las fórmulas de tratamiento, pero se forman con la tercera persona.

OBJETO DIRECTO

	singular	plural
1º persona	me	nos
2º persona	te	os
3º persona	le/lo/la	los/las

OBJETO INDIRECTO

	singular	plural
1º persona	me	nos
2º persona	te	os
3º persona	le	les

COLOCACIÓN DE LOS PRONOMBRES PERSONALES OBJETO

Se colocan siempre delante del verbo:

> • **Lo** veo desde la ventana.

excepto cuando el verbo está en *imperativo afirmativo* que va detrás del verbo y forma una palabra.

> • Da**le** dos a tu hermano.

Con las perífrasis de *infinitivo* y *gerundio* pueden ir detrás o delante:

- ¿Puede decir**me** dónde está la plaza Cataluña?
- ¿**Me** puede **decir** dónde está la plaza Cataluña?

- Está preparándo**la**.
- **La** está **preparando**.

Cuando en el discurso aparecen dos pronombres objeto (objeto directo e indirecto) juntos, el pronombre objeto indirecto se coloca delante del objeto directo.

- ¿**Me lo** das?
- ¿Puedes dár**melo**?
- Dá**melo**.
- Estoy preparándo**sela**.

El pronombre objeto indirecto **le-les** cambia por **se** cuando se encuentra delante de **le/lo/la/los/las**:

- ¿**Se lo** doy?
- ○ Sí, dá**selo.**

LOS PRONOMBRES CON PREPOSICIONES

1° persona	mí
2° persona	ti

Los pronombres **yo** y **tu** acompañados de preposición cambian a **mí** y **ti**:

- Toma. Esto es **para ti.**
- ○ ¿**Para mí?** ¡Qué sorpresa!

Para el resto de las personas se usa la preposición seguida de las formas del pronombre personal sujeto:

- Hay un recado en el contestador **para vosotros.**
- Este libro es **para él**.

La preposición **con** tiene una construcción especial con los pronombres personales de primera y segunda persona singular:

con +	mí	....	conmigo
	ti	....	contigo

- ¿Vienes **conmigo** al cine?

Con las demás personas se usa el pronombre personal sujeto:

- ¿Fue Lucía al cine con Javi?
- ○ Claro que fue **con él,** ¿con quién va a ir?
- **Con nosotros** nunca quiere venir.

LOS PRONOMBRES REFLEXIVOS

Se refieren al sujeto de la oración y se colocan delante de las formas personales del verbo.

	singular	plural
1° persona	me	nos
2° persona	te	os
3° persona	se	se

Con las formas de *imperativo* y con las no personales de *infinitivo* y *gerundio* se colocan detrás, formando una palabra:

- Vís**te**, que ya es tarde para el colegio.
- Ven a lavar**te**.

- ¿Y la niña? ¿Dónde está la niña?
- Bañándo**se**.

Con las perífrasis pueden colocarse detrás del *infinitivo* o *gerundio,* o delante del *verbo auxiliar:*

- **Tengo que** arreglar**me** para salir.
- **Me tengo que** arreglar para salir.

- **¿Qué** haces?
- **Estoy** vistiéndo**me**./
  Me estoy vistiendo.

Estas formas acompañan siempre a *verbos reflexivos* (**vestirse, lavarse, bañarse, peinarse**) y a otros que sin serlo pueden actuar como tales (**irse, marcharse, salirse**).

- **Me** voy, es tarde.

LOS NUMERALES

Los numerales se utilizan para cuantificar.

Generalmente acompañan al sustantivo (adjetivos) pero también aparecen solos (pronombres).

NUMERALES CARDINALES

0 cero	11 once	30 treinta
1 uno	12 doce	31 treinta y uno
2 dos	13 trece	40 cuarenta
3 tres	14 catorce	50 cincuenta
4 cuatro	15 quince	60 sesenta
5 cinco	16 dieciséis	70 setenta
6 seis	17 diecisiete	80 ochenta
7 siete	18 dieciocho	90 noventa
8 ocho	19 diecinueve	100 cien
9 nueve	20 veinte	101 ciento uno
10 diez	21 veintiuno	

200	doscientos	/-as
300	trescientos	/-as
400	cuatrocientos	/-as
500	quinientos	/-as
600	seiscientos	/-as
700	setecientos	/-as
800	ochocientos	/-as
900	novecientos	/-as

1.000	mil
2.000	dos mil
...	
1.000.000	un millón

Uno puede ser masculino o femenino según el género del sustantivo al que acompaña o sustituye. **Uno** delante del sustantivo masculino singular se apocopa **un**:

- Nosotros tenemos **un** hijo.
- Sólo tienen **una** hija.

NUMERALES ORDINALES

Varían en género y número según el sustantivo al que acompañan o sustituyen.

primero	/-a	1° / 1^a
segundo	/-a	2° / 2^a
tercero	/-a	3° / 3^a
cuarto	/-a	4° / 4^a
quinto	/-a	5° / 5^a
sexto	/-a	6° / 6^a
séptimo	/-a	7° / 7^a
octavo	/-a	8° / 8^a
noveno	/-a	9° / 9^a
décimo	/-a	10° / 10^a

Pueden ir delante o detrás del sustantivo:

piso **quinto** / **quinto** piso

excepto con los nombres de reyes y papas:

Juan Pablo II (**segundo**)

Primero y **tercero** se apocopan delante del sustantivo masculino singular:
primer día / día **primero**
tercer piso /piso **tercero**

LOS INDEFINIDOS

Expresan contenidos de carácter numérico o cuantitativo y dan una significación vaga e imprecisa.
Los indefinidos pueden funcionar como adjetivos, pronombres y adverbios.

ADJETIVOS Y PRONOMBRES INDEFINIDOS

Los *indefinidos adjetivos* acompañan al sustantivo:

- Lo he visto en **varias** ocasiones.

Y los *indefinidos pronombres* sustituyen al nombre:

- No se ha comprado **ninguno.**

❑ **Uno/a/os/as**

- He tenido **unos** días agitados.

❑ **Alguno/a/os/as** (*afirmativo*)

- Tengo **algunos** meses de vacaciones.

❑ **Ninguno/a/os/as** (*negativo*)

- Allí no tenemos **ninguna.**

❑ **Todo/a/os/as**

- **Todos** han salido.

❑ **Algo** (*neutro afirmativo*)

- ¿Ves **algo?**

❑ **Nada** (*neutro negativo*)

- No veo **nada.**

❑ **Mucho/a/os/as**

- Tienen **muchos** libros.

❏ **Demasiado/a/os/as**

> • Ha puesto **demasiadas** flores.

❏ **Bastante/es**

> • No tienen **bastante** tiempo.

❏ **Poco/a/os/as**

> • Lee **pocos** (libros de arte).

❏ **Alguien** (*para personas afirmativo*)

> • ¿Hay **alguien?**

❏ **Nadie** (*para personas negativo*)

> • No, no hay **nadie.**

❏ **Varios/as**

> • **Varias** personas me han preguntado por ti.

❏ **Otro/a/os/as**

> • ¿Quieres **otro?**

❏ **Cada +** *sustantivo*

> • **Cada día** sale de casa a las 8.

ADVERBIOS INDEFINIDOS

Los adverbios indefinidos acompañan a verbos (postpuestos) o a adjetivos (antepuestos).

mucho/muy	poco
demasiado	bastante
nada	algo

• No he comido **nada.**
• Esa película es **bastante** interesante.

LOS PRONOMBRES INTERROGATIVOS Y EXCLAMATIVOS

PRONOMBRES INTERROGATIVOS

Los pronombres interrogativos sirven para preguntar sobre una información desconocida para el hablante. Todos estos pronombres llevan acento gráfico.

Las oraciones interrogativas pueden ser directas o indirectas. En las *interrogativas directas* el pronombre se sitúa al principio de la oración, y la oración lleva signos de interrogación (¿?).

En la *indirecta* el pronombre ocupa el lugar de la información desconocida, y va sin los signos de interrogación:

- Le pregunté **dónde** vivía.
- No sabía **cuándo** iba a llegar.
- El no tenía ni idea de **cómo** vendría.

qué, cuándo, cómo, dónde, quién/-es, cuál/-es, cuánto/-a/-os/-as	+ *verbo*

- ¿**Qué** quieren tomar?
- ¿**Cuándo** sales de viaje?
- ¿**Dónde** vive tu familia?
- ¿**Quiénes** van de excursión?
- ¿**Cuál** es tu chaqueta?
- ¿**Cómo** te llamas?
- ¿**Cuánto** vale?

qué cuánto/-a/-os/-as	+ *sustantivo*

- ¿**Qué coche** te has comprado?
- ¿**Cuántos hermanos** tienes?

> **cuál + de** + *sustantivo/pronombre*

- ¿**Cuál de los libros** te has leído?
- ¿**Cuál de ellos** viene hoy?

CONTRASTE QUÉ/CUÁL + VERBO

Qué se utiliza en preguntas de tipo general sobre algo de lo que el hablante no tiene información previa.

- ¿**Qué quieres?**
- ○ Un libro.

Cuál se utiliza en preguntas en las que se quiere identificar uno/s entre los componentes de un grupo de los que se tiene información previa.

- Tengo un libro de Cervantes, otro de Quevedo y de Lope, ¿**cuál quieres?**
- ○ El de Cervantes.

PRONOMBRES EXCLAMATIVOS

Los pronombres exclamativos se utilizan para expresar la afectividad del hablante. Las formas de los pronombres son las mismas que las de los pronombres interrogativos acompañados de los signos de exclamación (¡!):

- ¡**Qué** camisa tan bonita!
- ¡**Cuánta** gente en la misma habitación!
- ¡**Cómo** lo hicieron! Fue maravilloso.

LOS PRONOMBRES RELATIVOS

El pronombre relativo se refiere a una palabra conocida por el hablante (antecedente) que puede ser un sustantivo, un pronombre, un adjetivo, un adverbio o una frase completa. El antecedente puede estar presente o no en el discurso.

> **que, quien/-es, cual/-es, cuyo/-a/-os/-as, cuanto/-a/-os/-as, donde, como, cuando**

PRONOMBRES RELATIVOS CON ANTECEDENTE EXPLÍCITO

❑ Que

El antecedente puede ser persona o cosa:

- Mira, *aquella chica* **que** está en la puerta es mi vecina.
- ¿Ya te has comprado *el libro* **que** me dijiste?

El pronombre **que** puede ir precedido de *artículo* (**el/ la/ los/ las**) y/o de *preposición:*

- El colegio **en el que** estudia está muy lejos de casa.
- Juan, **el que** te llamó el otro día, te ha vuelto a llamar.
- Recuerdo muy bien el día **en que** se casó mi hija.

❑ Quien/-es

El antecedente sólo puede ser persona y puede ir precedido de *preposición:*

- *El señor* **con quien** está hablando la secretaria es el director de la escuela.
- *Los chicos* **quienes** aprueben el examen tienen que pasar por la Secretaría.

❑ Cual/-es

El antecedente puede ser persona o cosa, va precedido de *artículo* (**el/la/los/las**) y puede ir acompañado de *preposición:*

- *La empresa* **para la cual** trabajaba ha abierto una sucursal en Toledo.
- Estos son *los tres chicos* **para los cuales** pedí la beca.

❑ **Cuyo/-a/-os/-as**

El antecedente puede ser persona o cosa, concuerda en género y número con el sustantivo que le sigue y puede ir precedido de preposición. Se utiliza para indicar propiedad en los registros literarios. Equivale a **de quien/-es, del que/de los que, del cual/de los cuales.**

- Es un *político* **cuyas ideas** no comparto.
- El *chico*, **cuyo padre** es arquitecto, es un fuera de serie.

❑ **Cuanto/-a/-os/-as**

El antecedente puede ser persona o cosa y concuerda en género y número.

- *Las manzanas* que hay en el cesto son de nuestro huerto, puedes coger **cuantas** quieras.

❑ **Donde**

El antecedente es un lugar, puede ir acompañado de preposición.

- *La carretera* **por donde** circulamos es comarcal.
- Este es *el lugar* **(en) donde** lo encontré.

❑ **Cuando**

El antecedente es un elemento temporal.

- Fue el *tres de abril* **cuando** salimos de viaje.

❑ **Como**

Tiene valor modal.

- Esta ciudad es **como** me la había imaginado.

EL ADVERBIO

❏ El adverbio califica o determina a:

verbo: Come **mucho**.
adjetivo: Es **muy** inteligente.
participio: Está **bien** preparado.
adverbio: Mi casa está **bastante** lejos.

❏ El adverbio es invariable en género y número:

• Come **mucho**. / Comen **mucho**.
• La niña es **muy** lista. / El niño es **muy** listo.

CLASES DE ADVERBIOS

❏ Adverbios calificativos: **rápidamente, mal, bien, peor, mejor**...

• Esta chica canta **bien**.
• Todo lo hace **rápidamente**.

❏ Adverbios de cantidad: **muy, mucho, bastante, todo, nada, menos, sólo**...

• Este mes trabajamos **menos**.
• **Sólo** tengo mil pesetas.

❏ Adverbios de lugar: **aquí, ahí, arriba, abajo, dentro, fuera, lejos**...

• ¿La calle Mayor está por **aquí**?
◦ No, cae **lejos**.

❏ Adverbios de tiempo: **ayer, hoy, mañana, nunca, pronto, tarde**...

• No te preocupes, llegaré **pronto**.
• La fiesta no es **hoy**, es **mañana**.

❏ Adverbios de afirmación: **sí, también, verdaderamente**...

• Me gusta mucho el pescado.
◦ A mí **también**. Sobre todo para cenar.

❏ Adverbios de negación: **no, nunca, jamás, tampoco**...

• Yo **nunca** como carne, **no** me gusta.
◦ A mí **tampoco**. Es como muy seca.

❑ Adverbios de duda: **quizá, tal vez, seguramente**...

> • **Quizá** lo he visto pero no lo recuerdo.
> • **Seguramente** vendrá mañana.

❑ Adverbios en **-mente**: se forman a partir de un adjetivo, añadiendo al femenino la terminación -mente:

| verdadero | ➞ | **verdaderamente** |
| limpio | ➞ | **limpiamente** |

También pueden sustituirse por: **con** + *nombre*

| tranquilamente | ➞ | **con tranquilidad** |
| cuidadosamente | ➞ | **con cuidado** |

POSICIÓN

❑ Los adverbios de tiempo y de lugar pueden colocarse delante o detrás del verbo:

> • **Mañana** voy. — Voy **mañana.**
> • Pedro vive **aquí.** — **Aquí** vive Pedro.

❑ Los adverbios de negación (**tampoco, nunca, jamás**) se colocan al principio de la frase:

> • **Nunca** llegará.

Si se colocan detrás del verbo se usa **no... nunca**:

> • **No** llegará **nunca.**

❑ Los adverbios **muy** y **bastante** se colocan antes del adjetivo, participio o adverbio:

> • El frigorífico está **bastante** estropeado.
> • Este diccionario resulta **muy** útil.

APÓCOPE

Los adverbios **tanto** y **mucho** se apocopan en **tan** y **muy** cuando van delante del adjetivo, participio o adverbio.

> • ¡Qué conferencia **tan** interesante! Lo ha hecho **muy** bien.

LA PREPOSICIÓN

La preposición es la partícula invariable que sirve para unir palabras y establecer una relación entre ellas.

> a - ante - bajo - cabe - con - contra - de - desde - en - entre -
> hacia - hasta - para - por - según - sin - sobre - tras

USOS DE LAS PREPOSICIONES

A

❑ Dirección y movimiento:

- Voy **a** Santander.

❑ Finalidad:

- Le compró un regalo **a** su madre.
- Voy **a** trabajar en seguida.

❑ Referencia temporal:

- Estaré allí **a** las siete y media.

❑ Referencia espacial:

- Te espera **a** la puerta del cine.

❑ Modo:

- Tortilla **a** la española.

CON

❑ Compañía:

- ¿Vives **con** tu novio?

❑ Instrumento:

- Tienes que escribirlo **con** bolígrafo.

CONTRA

❑ Oposición:

> • Ayer jugó el Real Madrid **contra** el Milán.

DE

❑ Posesión:

> • Hemos vendido la casa **de** mis padres.

❑ Materia:

> • Le han regalado un reloj **de** oro.

❑ Origen:

> • El tren de Sevilla lleva media hora **de** retraso.

❑ Tiempo:

> • Trabaja **de** noche y duerme **de** día.

DESDE

❑ Expresa el inicio de algo, el punto de partida en el espacio y en el tiempo:
> • Estoy aquí **desde** las ocho.

❑ Se utiliza en correlación con hasta (**desde ...hasta**):
> • Va a pie **desde** su casa hasta la oficina.

EN

❑ Lugar:

> • Deja los libros **en** la estantería.

❑ Medio:

> • No iré **en** coche, iré **en** tren.

❑ Modo/ manera:

> • Habla **en** broma.

❑ Situación en el tiempo:

> • **En** agosto estuve de vacaciones.

ENTRE

❑ Reciprocidad:

> • Lo podemos hacer **entre** los dos, será más fácil.

❑ Espacio de tiempo:

> • **Entre** hoy y mañana tengo que hacer los ejercicios.

HACIA

❑ Lugar y tiempo aproximado:

> • Llega **hacia** las tres.
> • Me dirijo **hacia** el centro de la ciudad.

HASTA

❑ Expresa el término de algo tanto en el espacio como en el tiempo:

> • No lo sabremos **hasta** el sábado.
> • Tienes que escribir **hasta** la página 32.

❑ Se utiliza en correlación con **desde** (desde.... hasta):

> • Fue corriendo **desde** aquí **hasta** la plaza.

POR

❑ Causa o motivo:

> • Trabajo **por** necesidad.

❑ Período de tiempo:

> • **Por** la mañana. / **Por** la tarde. / **Por** la noche.

excepto:

> • **A** mediodía. / **A** medianoche.

❑ Lugar aproximado:

> • Tiene la tienda **por** la zona norte de la ciudad.

❑ Cambio:

> • Cambio dólares **por** pesetas.

❑ Medio:

> • Llámale **por** teléfono.

❑ Precio:

> • Lo compré **por** mil pesetas.

❑ **Estar + por +** *infinitivo:*

> • La comida **está por** *hacer.*

❑ Equivalente a "a través de":

> • Cruza **por** el parque.

PARA

❑ Finalidad o destino:

> • Toma, esto es **para** ti.

❑ Dirección:

> • Ayer salió **para** Francia.

❑ Término de tiempo:

> • Tienes que terminarlo **para** el lunes.

❑ **Estar + para +** *infinitivo* = "estar a punto de" :

> • Cuando llegué **estaba para** *salir.*

ANTE - "delante de":

> • Se sentó **ante** él y le habló en voz baja.

BAJO - "debajo de":

> • Nos tumbamos **bajo** el manzano.

SIN - (opuesto a **con**):

> • Estoy **sin** dinero.

SOBRE - "encima de / alrededor de":

> • Tienes la llave **sobre** la mesa de la cocina.
> • Llegaré **sobre** las 8.

TRAS - "detrás de":

> • En cuanto lo vio, corrió **tras** él.

LA CONJUNCIÓN

La conjunción es la partícula invariable que sirve para unir palabras y oraciones.

CLASES DE CONJUNCIONES

Las conjunciones pueden ser:

- *coordinantes*: cuando unen dos elementos en la oración o dos oraciones que tienen significación completa.

> • El padre **y** la madre son australianos.
> • Ella habló **y** todos nos callamos.

- *subordinantes*: cuando unen dos oraciones que sólo estando juntas tienen significado completo. Una oración es la que da la información, la oración principal, la otra oración es la que va introducida por una conjunción, la oración subordinada*.

> • Te lo compraré   **si**   me das el dinero.
>
>   oración principal + conjunción + oración subordinada

COORDINANTES

❑ Copulativas: unen elementos que tienen relación entre ellos.

> **y (e), ni, que**

> • Escribe el nombre **y** la dirección.

❑ Adversativas: unen elementos que se oponen entre sí.

> **mas, pero, sino, sin embargo**

> • Tengo dinero **pero** no quiero comprarlo.

❑ Disyuntivas: expresan qué hay que elegir entre los elementos que unen.

> **o (u), ya, bien**

> • ¿Estudias **o** trabajas?

❑ Distributivas: unen elementos que alternan pero que no se excluyen.

> **ora...ora, ya...ya, sea...sea, bien...bien**

> • Iré a verte **ya sea** por la mañana **ya sea** por la tarde.

* ver "Usos del subjuntivo"

SUBORDINANTES

❑ Temporales: introducen oraciones que señalan referencias temporales para situar la acción. La relación temporal puede indicar anterioridad, simultaneidad o posterioridad.

> **cuando, en cuanto, mientras, hasta que, después de que, tan pronto como**

- Llámame **cuando** vuelvas de viaje.

❑ Concesivas: introducen oraciones que ponen una dificultad al cumplimiento de la oración principal.

> **aunque, por más (mucho) que, así, aun cuando, si bien, y eso que**

- Saldré **aunque** llueva.

❑ Finales: introducen oraciones que explican para qué se realiza la acción principal.

> **para que, a fin de que, a que, con el propósito de que, con el objeto de que, con el fin de que**

- Te lo digo **para que** lo sepas.

❑ Condicionales: introducen oraciones que ponen una condición para que se cumpla lo que dice la oración principal.

> **si, con tal (de) que, como si, como, con que, a menos que, siempre y cuando, a condición de que**

- **Si** viene me avisas.

❑ Causales: introducen oraciones que informan sobre la causa o motivo de que se produzca o no lo indicado en la oración principal.

> **porque, puesto que, pues, ya que, como, que**

- Lo compré **porque** me gustó.

❑ Consecutivas: introducen oraciones que expresan la consecuencia que se saca de lo que dice la oración principal.

> **ya que, con que, por (lo) tanto, así que, por consiguiente, por eso, de tal modo/forma que**

- **Ya que** vas, cómpralo tú.

❑ Modales: introducen oraciones que explican cómo se realiza la acción principal.

> **como, según**

- **Según** veas que transcurre la reunión, tomas una decisión u otra.

ORTOGRAFÍA

B y V /b/

La **b** y la **v** se **pronuncian** de la misma forma.

❏ Después de **m** siempre se escribe **b**:

cam**b**iar, em**b**arcar.

❏ Después de **n** siempre se escribe **v**:

en**v**iar, con**v**ocar.

❏ Se escribe **b** delante de otra *consonante:*

hom**b**re, **b**lanco.

❏ Se escriben con **b** los verbos cuyo *infinitivo* termina en **-bir:**

escri**bir**, prohi**bir**.

excepto: her**v**ir, ser**v**ir y vi**v**ir.

❏ Se escriben con **b** las palabras que comienzan por:

bibl-:	**bibl**ia
bu-:	**bu**taca
bur-:	**bur**guesía
bus-:	**bus**to

❏ Se escriben con **b** las palabras que terminan en:

-bilidad:	ama**bilidad**
-bundo:	vaga**bundo**
-bunda:	a**bunda**

excepto: mo**v**ilidad y ci**v**ilidad

❏ Se escriben con **v** las palabras que comienzan por **ad-**:

adverbio, **adv**erso.

❑ Se escriben con **v** los *adjetivos* acentuados en la penúltima sílaba que terminan en:

-ave:	gr**ave**
-avo:	oct**avo**
-eva:	nu**eva**
-eve:	l**eve**
-evo:	nu**evo**
-iva:	decis**iva**
-ivo:	act**ivo**

G, GU /g/

ga:	**ga**fas	**gue:**	**gue**rra
go:	**go**rro	**gui:**	**gui**tarra
gu:	**gu**sano		

En **gue** y **gui** la **u** no se pronuncia. En los casos en los que se pronuncia, la **u** se escribe con diéresis:

cig**ü**eña

ling**ü**ística

J, G /x/

ja:	**ja**món	**je, ge:**	**Je**rónimo, **ge**nte
jo:	**jo**ven	**ji, gi:**	**ji**rafa, **gi**rasol
ju:	**ju**rar		

❑ Se escriben con **j** las palabras terminadas en:

-aje :	gar**aje**
-eje :	her**eje**

❑ Se escriben con **j** las palabras que terminan en:

-jería : cerra**jería**

❑ Se escriben con **g** las palabras que comienzan en:

geo- : **geo**grafía

❑ Se escriben con **g** las palabras que terminan en:

- gen: ori**gen**

❑ Se escriben con **g** los *infinitivos* terminados en:

- **ger** : prote**ger**
- **gir** : ele**gir**

C, Q /k/

ca :	**ca**ra	**que** :	**que**rer
co :	**co**lor	**qui** :	**qui**nto
cu :	**cu**ello		

Qu se escribe sólo delante de **-e/-i** y nunca se pronuncia la **u**.

Z, C /θ/

za:	**Za**mora	**ze:**	**ze**ta
zo:	**zo**na	**ce:**	**ce**rrojo
zu:	**zu**eco	**zi:**	na**zi**
		ci:	**ci**nco

Ze y **zi** tienen poco uso y en algunos casos pueden escribirse con **c**:

zebra / **ce**bra
zinc / **ci**nc

Todas las palabras que terminan en **-z** hacen su plural en:

- **ces** : pe**z**/pe**ces**

H

No se pronuncia nunca.

Se escriben con **h** las palabras que comienzan en:

hue-:	**hue**vo
hidr- :	**hidr**ógeno
hiper- :	**hiper**mercado
hipo- :	**hipo**pótamo

ACENTUACIÓN

Las palabras en las que la carga acentual recae en la **última sílaba** se acentúan cuando terminan en:

vocal :	sof**á**
-n :	cañ**ó**n
-s :	jam**á**s

Las palabras cuya carga acentual recae en la **penúltima sílaba** se acentúan cuando terminan en:

consonante :	**á**rbol

excepto: las que terminan en:

-n:	exame**n**
-s:	tesi**s**

Las palabras cuya carga acentual recae en la **antepenúltima sílaba** se acentúan todas:

tr**á**fico

Los monosílabos **no** se acentúan, excepto cuando existen dos iguales en su forma pero que tienen distinta función gramatical:

el	artículo	**él**	pronombre
mi	adjetivo posesivo	**mí**	pronombre personal
tu	adjetivo posesivo	**tú**	pronombre personal
mas	conjunción	**más**	adverbio
si	conjunción	**sí**	afirmación o pronombre reflexivo
de	preposición	**dé**	verbo dar
se	pronombre	**sé**	verbos saber y ser
aun	adverbio de cantidad	**aún**	adverbio de tiempo
te	pronombre	**té**	nombre

Los adverbios formados por *adjetivo* + *-mente* conservan el acento del adjetivo:

f**á**cil   —   f**á**cilmente

Llevan acento los pronombres y adverbios interrogativos y exclamativos: **qué, cuál, quién, cuánto, cuándo, cómo** y **dónde**.

Los pronombres demostrativos (**este, ese, aquel**...) llevan acento cuando pueden confundirse con los adjetivos demostrativos.

La palabra **solo** puede llevar acento cuando funciona como adverbio para evitar la confusión con **solo** adjetivo.

ÍNDICE

Índice